Unity
in Psychology

Unity
in Psychology

*Possibility or
Pipedream?*

Edited by Robert J. Sternberg

AMERICAN PSYCHOLOGICAL ASSOCIATION • *Washington, DC*

Published by
American Psychological Association
750 First Street, NE
Washington, DC 20002
www.apa.org

To order
APA Order Department
P.O. Box 92984
Washington, DC 20090-2984
Tel: (800) 374-2721
Direct: (202) 336-5510
Fax: (202) 336-5502
TDD/TTY: (202) 336-6123
Online: www.apa.org/books/
E-mail: order@apa.org

In the U.K., Europe, Africa, and the Middle East, copies may be ordered from
American Psychological Association
3 Henrietta Street
Covent Garden, London
WC2E 8LU England

Typeset in Goudy by World Composition Services, Inc., Sterling, VA

Printer: United Book Press, Inc., Baltimore, MD
Cover Designer: Naylor Design, Washington, DC
Project Manager: Debbie Hardin, Carlsbad, CA

The opinions and statements published are the responsibility of the authors, and such opinions and statements do not necessarily represent the policies of the American Psychological Association.

Library of Congress Cataloging-in-Publication Data

Unity in psychology : possibility or pipedream? / edited by Robert J. Sternberg.
    p. cm.
Includes bibliographical references and indexes.
ISBN 1-59147-156-7
1. Psychology—Philosophy. I. Sternberg, Robert J.

BF38.U55   2004
150′.1′—dc22   2004003908

British Library Cataloguing-in-Publication Data
A CIP record is available from the British Library.

Printed in the United States of America
First Edition

This book is dedicated to the memory of William James,
the first great American unifier of psychology.

CONTENTS

CONTRIBUTORS

Charles L. Brewer, Furman University, Greenville, SC
Merry Bullock, American Psychological Association, Washington, DC
Florence L. Denmark, Pace University, New York
Daniel B. Fishman, Rutgers University, Piscataway, NJ
Raymond D. Fowler, American Psychological Association, Washington, DC
Howard Gardner, Harvard Graduate School of Education, Cambridge, MA
Gregory A. Kimble, Duke University, Durham, NC
Herbert H. Krauss, Pace University, New York
Ronald F. Levant, Nova Southeastern University, Ft. Lauderdale, FL
Thomas V. McGovern, Arizona State University West, Phoenix
Stanley B. Messer, Rutgers University, Piscataway, NJ
Joseph F. Rychlak, Loyola University, Chicago, IL
Arthur W. Staats, University of Hawaii, Honolulu
Robert J. Sternberg, Yale University, New Haven, CT

PREFACE

When my children were little, I once suggested we go out to eat. I asked them what restaurant they wanted to go to. Both kids were excited with this prospect. Seth insisted on going to one place, Sara on another. I suggested a compromise. No third restaurant would do. I suggested we go to one restaurant that day and another one some other day. They wouldn't hear of it. Eventually, I got disgusted. We ate at home.

At times, we psychologists are like Seth and Sara were when they were young children. Two or more groups of psychologists, each certain it is right in what it wants, insists on having things its own way. Ultimately, the groups all lose. None of them gets its way, and no one outside these groups wishes to pay attention anymore. Like Seth and Sara that day, opposing interest groups within our field can end up "cutting off their nose to spite their face."

The goal of this book is to examine the opportunities for psychology to become unified in the face of increasing fragmentation. The motivation for the book is to encourage psychologists to unify themselves before the field of psychology disappears as a unified field or before the field splits into many splinter groups and organizations that lose sight of the field of psychology as a whole.

I personally believe in unified psychology. The basic idea is simple: to acknowledge our differences but also to rise above them, especially in our dealings with the outside world.

There are several reasons why unity is important to us.

- *Conserving resources*: Opposing factions in conflictual organiza- tions end up consuming their resources fighting each other rather than fighting for the organization and its interests as a whole.

- *Credibility:* No one on the outside wants to listen to a group that cannot ultimately speak with a unified voice, anymore than I was willing to listen to Seth and Sara when each insisted on having his or her way. If we want to have the option of prescription privileges for psychologists or to get more money for research support, we will get nowhere if we do not speak with a unified voice. Quite simply, we will lack credibility.
- *Profiting from each other:* Groups that fight each other suffer rather than profit from the diversity they have to offer each other. We see this as well in countries where ethnic groups battle each other rather than work together.
- *Recognizing our interdependence:* We all need each other. Scientists need practitioners. Without practitioners, there would be few psychology students for scientists to teach (because most students, when all is said and done, are particularly interested in practice issues) and hence fewer university slots for psychologists; grant support would diminish as congressional representatives, whose main interest is in serving constituents' needs, would see less reason to fund psychological research; and there would be no one to use the results of our science to make a difference to the world. Without scientists, there would be few theories, fewer therapies, and little hard data on which practitioners could draw.
- *Asking the right questions:* When we become beholden to particular fields, methods, or paradigms, we often ask not the best question but instead the question that our allegiance "allows" us to ask. For example, instead of asking what is the absolute best way to treat a patient, we ask only which of the methods of our paradigm we should use. Or as another example, if we study memory but see ourselves only as "cognitive" psychologists, we fail to ask the interesting questions about memory that a biological psychologist, developmental psychologist, clinical psychologist, or educational psychologist might ask.
- *We're all the same at heart:* Great scientists have a style, like a good artist. Great therapists also have a style. They, too, practice in ways that draw on both science and art.

This book presents diverse viewpoints on unification. I hope you find the issues with which the authors deal as exciting as I do.

ACKNOWLEDGMENTS

I am grateful to Alejandro Isgut and Cheri Stahl for their assistance in the preparation of the manuscript for the book. I am also grateful to the funding agencies that have made spending time on this book possible. In particular, I thank the United States Army Research Institute for the Behavioral Sciences (Contract MDA903-92-K), the National Science Foundation (Grant REC-9979843), and the Javits Act Program (Grant R206R000001) as administered by the Institute of Education Sciences, U.S. Department of Education. Grantees undertaking such projects are encouraged to express freely their professional judgment. This publication, therefore, does not necessarily represent the position or policies of the National Science Foundation, Office of Educational Research and Improvement, or the U.S. Department of Education. Views and opinions expressed herein are solely those of the authors and do not represent the official view of the U.S. Military Academy, the U.S. Army, or any other agency of the U.S. government, and no official endorsement should be inferred.

Unity
in Psychology

1

UNIFYING THE
FIELD OF PSYCHOLOGY

ROBERT J. STERNBERG

Psychology is becoming increasingly specialized, and at the same time it is increasingly fragmented. The cost is psychology's potential loss of identity as a field. Should psychology become increasingly fragmented, or should we attempt to stop this fragmentation before it goes so far as to be irreversible?

In a series of articles, my colleagues and I have proposed a "unified psychology" that seeks to remedy the fragmentation and even the schisms to which psychology has been exposed (Sternberg, 2002; Sternberg & Grigorenko, 2001; Sternberg, Grigorenko, & Kalmar, 2001). My goal is to identify means by which psychology can achieve unity.

Preparation of this chapter was supported by Grant REC-9979843 from the U.S. National Science Foundation, a grant from the W. T. Grant Foundation, and the Javits Act Program (Grant no. R206R000001) as administered by the Office of Educational Research and Improvement, U.S. Department of Education. Grantees undertaking such projects are encouraged to express freely their professional judgment. This chapter, therefore, does not necessarily represent the position or policies of any of the sponsoring agencies, and no official endorsement should be inferred.

SOURCES OF FRAGMENTATION

Why has psychology become fragmented? I believe there are three main reasons.

- *Devaluing*. Many students are being trained in ways that, early on, emphasize extreme specialization. Students may come to devalue approaches that are different from their own, just as people often devalue other individuals, in general, who seem different from themselves. Sometimes, such devaluing is a part of a more general snobbery on the part of those who feel that their own approach is better than other people's.
- *Ignorance*. Many students are learning almost exclusively about things that seem immediately relevant to their own work. The result may be that these students never learn much about areas and approaches other than those within a narrow range. The students may then come to reject those things about which they know little.
- *Competitive agendas*. Psychologists sometimes find themselves competing with each other. Researchers may compete for journal space, grant funds, or acceptance of their particular point of view. Practitioners may compete for clients. Competition may lead psychologists to reject the offerings of others with whom they are competing as one way of promoting the wares they are offering to "sell."

THE COSTS OF FRAGMENTATION

"United we stand, divided we fall."

Sound reasoning underlies this aphorism. Whatever the reasons, psychology as a field only hurts itself in its fragmentation. Again, there are at least three reasons for this.

- *Internal fights sap morale*. A house divided is a house full of unhappy people. Who can feel whole if the group with which one identifies is fragmented?
- *Bickering consumes resources*. When we bicker, we deplete our own resources. The time and energy that could be put to productive use instead is put to fighting among ourselves.
- *Schisms reduce external credibility*. To the extent that psychology speaks with conflicting voices, it is less likely to be listened to by others. Indeed, it will be unclear to others even to whom to listen because no one will be clearly representing psychology.

WHY UNITY?

Unity rather than fragmentation is the sensible path for psychology to take. An analysis of several sources of division suggests that they make little sense. I will concentrate on four sources of division: the science–practice split, the teaching–research split, the basic–applied research split, and splits among subfields within psychology.

THE SCIENCE–PRACTICE SPLIT

Some psychologists who identify themselves as scientists eschew those who identify themselves as practitioners, and vice versa. But this split is founded on misunderstanding.

Scientists need practitioners. The reasons are multiple.

- *Students.* Without practice, there would be few students. The overwhelming majority of students who study psychology, especially at the undergraduate level, do so because they are interested in practice issues, such as the identities and characteristics of various psychological disorders and how people with psychological disorders can be helped. If these issues were not taught, many students would not take courses in psychology, resulting in decreased enrollments in psychology programs and decreased job opportunities for teachers and the many scientists who earn their livings teaching.
- *Grant funding.* Without practice, there would be little grant funding. Most legislators who propose and authorize spending for psychological research are likely to be much more interested in why their child has a reading disability, or their spouse is depressed, or their parent has Alzheimer's, than they are in questions of basic research without obvious applications to practice. Much of the money that goes to non-practice-related issues is an offshoot of the money that goes to practice-related issues. Without the first, we would not have the second.
- *Application.* Without practice, there would be little application for the psychological research that is done. Ultimately, many people who enter psychology, even those who are scientists, care about people and their problems, and would like, sooner or later, for their research to have application in helping people with their problems. Practice provides a major vehicle for application.

Practice also needs science, however. Again, there are several reasons.

- *Theory*. Without science, many of the theories that are used by practitioners never would have been proposed. These theories are, or at least should be, scientific, meaning that they provide predictions and are capable of being disconfirmed. If they are not scientific, they are of dubious use, because there will be no empirical way of disconfirming them.
- *Assessment*. Without science, there would be few useful assessments. Assessments of intelligence, personality, and other attributes, for example, are useful only if they have been formulated through, or at least subjected to, rigorous scientific scrutiny. Without such scrutiny, one cannot know whether the assessments are of value.
- *Therapy*. Without science, there would be no adequate tests of therapies and perhaps few therapies at all. Clients spend a substantial amount of time and often money for therapy. They are entitled to some assurance that the therapy they receive is a good value for their investments of time and money.

In short, science and practice need each other. To heal a split, one must first understand why it has come about. My own understanding of the split has derived primarily from my work in the American Psychological Association (APA), first as president-elect and then as president.

Unintended Consequences of Free Speech

When academics have an argument, the argument is, well, academic. The consequences of who wins are notably small. Except in the rarest of instances, no one loses significant income, for example, because they have lost an academic argument. What they are most likely to lose is face; nothing more.

The same cannot be said for practice. The stakes of arguments can be very high. Suppose, for example, that one brand of psychotherapy is labeled as a fraud or merely as ineffective. Then practitioners of this therapy stand to lose not only their claim to professional integrity but also to income from clients.

Evidence-Based Practice

A current debate between some academics and some practitioners is over the notion of evidence-based practice. Certain clinical scientists are adamant that practice techniques that are not empirically verified are no more ethical than medicines administered to humans without empirical tests of their effectiveness. From their point of view, just as we would not give a new medication with unknown efficacy and side effects to a medical patient, so should we not try out unverified therapeutic techniques with clients of therapy.

Some practitioners—and, no doubt, some scientists as well—disagree with this position. They argue that it is and always will be impossible to try out every possible technique under every circumstance under which it might be administered. From their point of view, the number of possible situations that can arise is essentially infinite, and it will be a long, long time before science can ever give practitioners some kind of grand imprimatur for whatever they do. In the meantime, there are clients out there waiting to be helped, and they cannot wait for science to catch up with practice, just in case it ever will, which many of them view as doubtful.

There would seem to be a sensible middle road to compromise, but exactly where this middle road lies is not totally clear. For example, one might try out techniques on broad classes of therapeutic endeavors, such as treatments for depression, in general, and then generalize from whatever data are obtained. There is a problem with this strategy, however. Even a single global diagnosis has numerous subtypes and multiple manifestations within those subtypes. There are a number of different types of depression, for example, and even within a given type of depression, the presenting circumstances can be quite different. Will there ever be an adequate substitute for clinical judgment in such complex circumstances?

The answer depends, of course, on whom you ask. Some scientifically oriented clinical psychologists would say that, yes, we can obtain some reasonable degree of generalization from carefully selecting our cases to be representative of the population as a whole. Some clinicians would question whether the term *representative* has any clear meaning in this context. The result can be a stalemate, whereby neither side convinces the other, or even, ultimately, really tries.

I believe that a reasonable solution does involve some splitting of the difference. I agree with scientists that using techniques that have no or minimal empirical verification, or even for which there is strong reason to believe that they will be ineffective, is not justifiable. But neither is doing nothing in the absence of clearly relevant scientific data. Therapists need to seek as much empirical justification as possible for what they do, but not fail to act when the information is not as good as they would hope. At the same time, there is no excuse whatsoever for using techniques that have no scientific basis at all—Tarot cards, crystals, orgone boxes, and the like. We can only hope we are well beyond this ilk of practice.

Prescription Privileges

There are several reasons why psychologists ought to have the option of prescription privileges (see also Sternberg, 2001).

- *Treating the whole person.* Psychologists, like other professionals, once viewed physical and psychological disorders as relatively distinct. No longer. We now know that physical and psychological symptoms are highly interactive. Some practicing psychologists may believe, therefore, that to treat the whole person, they need to supplement psychotherapy with medications. Indeed, the biopsychosocial model adopted by many psychologists is consistent with an integration of kinds of treatments.
- *Providing "full service."* Psychologists would like to help their clients in as many ways as possible. Drugs provide one way among many.
- *Dependence on medical practitioners.* At the present time, psychologists may find themselves dependent on medical practitioners who have prescriptive authority. This dependence may increase costs and the time it takes to get clients drugs they may need.
- *Demonstrated success of prescriptive authority.* The U.S. Armed Forces devised a successful program for training psychologists to prescribe effectively and safely. An elite group of specially trained psychologists now has prescription privileges in the military.
- *Political feasibility.* The passage of a prescriptive-authority bill for psychologists in New Mexico shows that efforts to obtain prescriptive authority can in fact pay off.
- *Availability of practitioners.* In some locales, there simply are too few psychiatrists available. In these places it is especially important that psychologists be able to prescribe. This problem may worsen. Whereas psychology is a growing profession, psychiatry appears not to be.
- *Dual purpose.* Part of prescriptive authority may actually be a matter of psychologists' taking clients *off* medications prescribed by other kinds of professionals that are not effective or that actually are detrimental.
- *Economic well-being.* Practicing psychologists' incomes are being mercilessly squeezed by managed-care companies. They need every resource they can find to increase their incomes. The long-term economic well-being of the field may be tied in with prescriptive authority.

- *Faith in ourselves.* For whatever problems there may be with prescriptive authority, we need to have faith in ourselves—that when we are granted prescriptive authority, we will use it in a caring and responsible way.

I realize that many responsible psychologists are not in favor of prescriptive authority and that they believe they have perfectly good arguments for their view that prescriptive authority is a mistake. I would like to respond to at least some of these arguments.

- *Psychologists cannot duplicate the thorough training of medical doctors.* The argument is that no matter how much training psychologists receive, they still will not have received training comparable to that received by medical doctors. And if there is an underlying medical condition, they may be completely unaware of it. There are several potential rebuttals. First, no one is expecting psychologists to prescribe *all* drugs. The goal of the prescription-authority movement is authority for psychoactive drugs, not for drugs that, for example, treat blood clots. Second, just as doctors frequently refer patients to specialists when the problems the patients face go beyond their expertise, so can and should psychologists. Third, many of the decisions MDs make regarding dosages and drug interactions are done today through the use of hand-held computers, not on the basis of knowledge stored in the head. Psychologists can use these computers as well as MDs can.
- *The drug companies will take over the APA.* This is a legitimate worry. Recommendations are needed to combat this potential problem.
- *There is no time in the doctoral curriculum for such training.* I agree. Such training should be postdoctoral.
- *Use of drugs will crowd out and potentially eventually eliminate the practice of psychotherapy.* Some would argue that this has already happened to a large extent in psychiatry. Therapists can themselves become so dependent on drugs—that is, on prescribing them—that they practice little psychotherapy in conjunction with their administration. Some would argue that psychologists are somehow different. I suspect that they are not all so different. The same could happen to psychologists as has happened to some psychiatrists. Psychologists therefore need to be cautious to avoid this.

Is there any intermediate position that might help to promote unification? I believe there is. Prescription privileges have been tried, with success, in the military. They can have success in the civilian sector as well. Guam and New Mexico have passed bills that will allow psychologists to have prescription privileges under certain conditions. These two venues will provide test cases of psychologists' readiness to prescribe safely and effectively. I would like to see a systematic evaluation of the success of the program be conducted by a research organization that has no particular stake in the outcome. If, as I expect, the outcome is successful, then this success would be an indication that fears about granting prescriptive authority are unwarranted. However, if it is not a success, it would not mean that such a program *cannot* be a success. Rather, it would indicate that the terms under which prescriptive authority is granted need to be modified to some degree.

THE TEACHING–RESEARCH SPLIT

Sometimes teaching and research are pitted against each other. Such a manufactured opposition is foolish.

Teaching helps research in numerous ways:

- *Source of ideas*. Many of the best ideas occur to us when we get feedback from our students or when, in teaching something, we come to see it in a different light.
- *Source of participants*. We may obtain research participants through subject pools, through curiosity, or simply for pay in the context of universities.
- *Laboratory for trying out many of the ideas that arise from research.* Many researchers first try out their ideas on their students before subjecting them to the more formal process of peer review.

Likewise, research helps teaching:

- *Content for much of what we teach.* Without research, the field would stagnate and we would have little new to offer to students over the course of the years.
- *Experiential basis for teaching.* What researcher has not found that he or she is in a better position to teach about something if he or she is doing or has done research in that area? Research provides first-hand rather than second-hand knowledge about an area.
- *Passion for teaching.* Many teachers find that they are most passionate in their teaching about the areas in which they do research.

In summary, teaching and research are synergistic, not opposed. They should not be viewed as in opposition to one another. Then why do some people view them as being in opposition?

I believe that, where they are viewed as being in opposition, there are several motivating causes.

- *Fear*. Some professors who have spent their lives essentially teaching and doing little or no research may be afraid of changing norms that, in some universities, will require them to do research. They may view these new norms as threatening their sense of competence or the competence they will be perceived to have, and therefore argue that doing research will interfere with their teaching. Such an argument has little merit other than one of protecting an entrenched system.
- *Time*. A legitimate argument, I believe, is that professors have only limited time, and they cannot do everything. It is unfair to expect—as some universities appear to—that they teach a heavy load of courses, such as four or five per term, and also that they have an active program of research. In universities that emphasize research productivity and competence almost exclusively in promotions, essentially the opposite conclusion may be reached—that spending more time on teaching will crowd out research productivity and potentially cost one one's job.
- *Mission*. Some professors argue that the missions of teaching and research are potentially incompatible—that the mission of research is to create knowledge and the mission of teaching is to transmit it. One cannot expect the same people to accomplish both missions. I would argue, however, that the opposite is true. Researchers always have to communicate their findings through publication, conference presentations, and the like. There is no reason that they cannot communicate their research to students as well as to professionals. One might argue that, unlike teachers, researchers need communicate only the results of their own research, not that of other people. But this is not the case. A good scientific presentation always puts one's own work in the context of others'.

It is difficult not to be sympathetic to sides of these arguments. When expectations are placed on individuals that they simply cannot meet, they can end up doing their jobs poorly or, at the extreme, not at all. The problem is not an inherent conflict between teaching and research, however. Rather, it is in inflated expectations by administrators of what professors can accomplish.

It might be said that teachers, especially at liberal arts colleges, need to be generalists. Often, they will teach introductory psychology courses and other courses that appeal to nonmajors as well as majors. Moreover, they may need to teach courses in far-flung areas, if their departments are small and there cannot possibly be a specialist in each area of psychology. Researchers, this line of argument goes, need to be specialists, especially in an era when psychological knowledge is becoming more and more specialized. This argument maintains that the generalists and the specialists are two different kinds of people.

I believe that if we are reaching a point where all researchers are specialists without substantial knowledge of general psychology and of issues outside their areas of specialization, then we are in trouble as a field. Much of the best research in psychology has crossed areas, such as that of Nobel Prize winners Herbert Simon and Daniel Kahneman, which crosses psychology and economics, and often it has challenged conventional psychological notions.

THE BASIC–APPLIED RESEARCH SPLIT

The split between basic and applied research is foolish, in my opinion.

- *Basic research exists, in large part, to serve as a basis for later applied research.* For example, personality tests that are widely used today emerged out of basic research.
- *Applied research, in turn, often helps provide ideas for basic research.* For example, many of our theories of intelligence arose from the use of intelligence testing in practical applications. The two kinds of research should work in synchrony with, not in opposition to, each other.

Again, to understand the nature of the split, one has to understand some of the motivations behind it.

- *Elitism.* Some basic researchers are, quite simply, elitist. They would not sully themselves with the thought of applied research. They perpetuate a negative stereotype of science that has no place in psychology.
- *Short-term economic gains.* Some psychological research is done in venues that emphasize short-term profits. Managers may see little or no benefit in basic research, preferring to fund only the short-term applied research that leads to quick products and financial gain. In the long run, however, such research programs tend to exhaust themselves, because applied research so often emanates from basic research.

- *False perceptions*. There is a false perception among psychologists that applied research is necessarily atheoretical. This perception is simply incorrect. Applied research can be used for testing and implementing theories just as well as can be basic research.

In summary, there is no need for basic and applied research to be viewed as antithetical to each other. Rather, they complement each other.

SPLITS AMONG SUBFIELDS

Sometimes, we observe a separation or even mutual disdain among various fields of psychology. Biological psychologists may believe that their findings somehow are more basic or fundamental than the findings of other psychologists. Cognitive psychologists may believe that, when all is said and done, many of the problems studied by other fields, such as social and clinical psychology, are actually cognitive at their base. Both kinds of psychologists may look down on clinical psychologists, whereas clinical psychologists may view their research as useful in a way that neither biological nor cognitive research is.

In the unified psychological approach, we argue that arbitrary breakdowns of subfields are often counterproductive (Sternberg & Grigorenko, 2001). We as psychologists should concentrate on psychological phenomena rather than subfields, and when we do, we find that almost all subfields are likely to have something important to say about these phenomena. Psychological phenomena such as memory, intelligence, prejudice, and aggression all can be studied from biological, cognitive, social, or clinical points of view. When we restrict ourselves to a single subfield as a basis for inquiry, we restrict our understanding.

CONCLUSION

The fragmentation of psychology is a mistake. We (Sternberg & Grigorenko, 2001) have suggested a "cure"—namely, unified psychology, an approach that emphasizes studying psychological phenomena from a variety of perspectives (Sternberg & Grigorenko, 2001). This is not a new idea. On the contrary, it has been around for many years. William James certainly was a unified psychologist! What is sad is that psychology has been so slow to adopt such an idea and that psychology has been moving in the direction of fragmentation rather than unity. It is time to reverse course and move together rather than apart.

REFERENCES

Sternberg, R. J. (2001). Prescription privileges for psychologists: A view from academe. *California Psychologist, 34*(10), 16–17.

Sternberg, R. J. (2002). In search of a unified field of psychology. *APS Observer 15*(9), 9–10, 49.

Sternberg, R. J., & Grigorenko, E. L. (2001). Unified psychology. *American Psychologist, 56,* 1069–1079.

Sternberg, R. J., Grigorenko, E. L., & Kalmar, D. A. (2001). The role of theory in unified psychology. *Journal of Theoretical and Philosophical Psychology, 21,* 99–117.

2

UNIFICATION THROUGH DIVERSITY

FLORENCE L. DENMARK AND HERBERT H. KRAUSS

As a discipline, psychology is successful by any standard applied to it. It is well established and well thought of. It is productive, influential, and popular. Each leg of the tripod on which it rests—knowledge creation, knowledge dissemination, and knowledge application—are strong and of proven durability.

The scope of psychology's intellectual ambitions are unmatched by any of its sister sciences. It aims to understand, it seems at times, the whole of the human condition and to prescribe for it appropriate action when amelioratives are called for. Not only are psychologists continually mining the discipline's core for valid, relevant, and important results, but they are operating at its periphery in areas that clearly overlap the interests of other disciplines. In fact, psychologists have made key contributions to the development of those borderlands—be they abutting the territory of the physical, biological, or social sciences—to say nothing of the humanities. Psychologists have made key contributions to neurosciences, cognitive sciences, economics, gender studies, linguistics, statistics, and so on. No one doubts that the discipline has contributed significantly to the understanding of the human condition, although there are, indeed, a great many differing ideas about specifically what its major contributions have been.

Although courses in psychology are sometimes taught in high schools, it is in the varied settings of postsecondary education that psychology comes into its own. At the undergraduate level, psychology has an important place in the curriculum as a major specialty, as a prerequisite for the pursuit of other specialties (e.g., speech therapy, education, and so on), as a general education requirement, as a distribution requirement option, and as an elective for the curious. In most institutions it is the most popular or among the most popular areas of study. It is so for a number of reasons. First, the field has enormous breadth. It holds something of interest for everyone. It has something to say about brain function and how we think, the relationship between stress and disease, how we develop, the best design for cockpit instrumentation, the most effective treatment of emotional dysfunction, gender comparisons, school violence, employee selection, how to package a product, the best hue for a fire engine's visibility, and so on. Second, the field holds promise to tell us much more. Third, a degree in psychology is a beginning step to a career path in the health care industry, the corporate world, or graduate school. No other area in the arts and sciences provides such abundant opportunity. Fourth, in most colleges and universities, it is possible to earn an undergraduate degree in psychology if one possesses only modest aptitude for mathematics and science, thereby making psychology a possible course of study for most.

A master's degree in the field increasingly allows the individual to apply psychological knowledge in contexts, ranging from the clinic to the classroom. As a consequence, it is an extremely popular degree. The range of opportunities open to those holding a doctorate is wider still. Many, especially those in academic institutions of higher learning and research institutes and laboratories, in addition to all else they may do, will be involved actively in knowledge creation. Their research and scholarly interests will be as diverse as the discipline itself. So broad is the stretch of psychology that some colleagues will ask whether what others are working on is indeed psychology. For some, the question will be "Isn't that really biology?" for others, "Isn't that philosophy?" and yet for others, "Whatever does that have to do with the human experience?"

Increasingly psychology is a practitioner's discipline. It is wise, for those who would ask otherwise, to bear in mind that since its founding psychology has always drawn to it not only those interested in understanding the human condition, broadly understood, but those interested in *changing* it. In fact, a good part of the original impetus behind the formation of the social sciences as a group comes from an interest in improving the lot of humanity. The physiocrats of the late 18th and 19th centuries, for example, wished to learn how to make the economic system better; they were not interested solely in knowledge for knowledge's sake.

Although some revel in it, the very success of the practitioner strains the discipline. To a degree, wherever a discipline contains both "basic" and "applied" interests there is tension. On one side stands a group of psychologists who consider themselves dedicated to the promulgation of psychological science and who view with some dismay the activities of practitioners who seem more concerned with the demands of the marketplace than the search for the "truth." On the other side stands an increasing majority of psychologists who see themselves ethically grappling with the complexities posed by life's issues and life's problems and using every appropriate means available to ameliorate them. Just as the first group believes that the second does not respect sufficiently the dictates of "science," the second considers the first indifferent if not indisposed to furthering the professional development of psychology. And each of these groups has been well educated in the disdain of each for the other. Neither group seems to recognize how useful each faction has been to the other, how interdependent they truly are. Nor do they seem able to acknowledge, one to the other, that all too often self-righteousness has served as a mask for the pursuit of narrow self-interest or self-preservation.

To a degree, each group has a valid point to make about the other. If psychology is to advance as a science, psychologists must come together into a community of truth seekers. Practice based on any other grounds than fact is, in the long run, likely to fail and bring disrepute to those who make unsustainable claims about its validity.

Understandably, psychology's many successes and achievements have not proved to be an unalloyed good. Along with accomplishment has come strain. Questions about psychology's range, methods, coherence, and ends have arisen and require reply, a not uncommon occurrence in the course of its development or, for that matter, that of any discipline making "truth claims" about matters of relevance.

THE UNIFICATION OF PSYCHOLOGY: AN OVERVIEW OF THE ARGUMENT

This chapter focuses on whether psychology might benefit from paradigmatic unification along the lines found in the "hard" sciences. It begins by reporting what a convenience sample of psychologists think of the prospect. The conclusion: A greater degree of unification of the discipline would be beneficial if it did not come at the expense of psychology's diversity. Next, psychology's history and roots are viewed. It is observed that from its origin, the discipline has had broad, complex, and expansive aims. Its development has been influenced and nurtured by differing intellectual streams; it is rooted in the humanities as well as the physical and biological sciences. Any attempt at paradigmatic unification that does not take this reality into account is likely to end poorly for the discipline. The chapter then proceeds to the recent report that the epistemology of these two intellectual traditions have been converging. It touches on the possibility that their synthesis may yet provide a unifying paradigm for psychology that does justice to it. It ends without certainty that this will happen.

AN ARGUMENT FOR PARADIGMATIC UNIFICATION

Discussion about the need for unification is not new in psychology. Psychologists have been talking about the relative benefits of unification and diversity for decades (e.g., Koch, 1963). However, questions about which approach toward unification would best serve the field have gained more prominence recently, even finding their way into the American Psychological Association's presidential election platforms (Yowm, 2003). Despite this increased attention we seem no closer to a consensus than before. This chapter explores one aspect of the current press for the unification of the discipline. It addresses whether psychology's success would be advanced if it were paradigmatic and whether this is an auspicious time for an attempt to make it so.

We believe Koch (1963) was correct when he argued that of the questions that can be asked of a science (and psychology is grounded, at least in part, in the belief that it ought be one), none are more important than those about the relationships among its chief fields of inquiry and those about its relationships with other disciplines concerned with overlapping areas of study. Perhaps the most fundamental questions of this type are those that inquire about what investigative and knowledge accumulation strategies will best advance the field.

The reasoning forwarded by proponents of the unification of psychology under one paradigm takes the following form. The most successful of sciences—that is, the natural and biological sciences—are mature sciences. Mature sciences are characteristically paradigmatic (Eysenck, 1997). Psychology, as it is currently, is too disorganized a field to be considered anything but preparadigmatic. In fact, there is no agreed on paradigm in any subfield of psychology (Eysenck, 1997). Because agreement on a paradigm is lacking in psychology (Staats, 1991, p. 910), psychology must, by definition, not be a science:

> No matter how many well-conducted experiments psychology produces,
> no matter the refinements of methods of data production and analysis,

no matter how sophisticated the specialized apparatus and theory construction, as long as psychology's products are inconsistent, unrelated and mutually discrediting, psychology will be considered a "would-be scientific discipline," a tangle of knowledge rather than a clear-cut field of science. (Staats, 1991, p. 910)

Unification is therefore necessary before psychology can be considered a unified science (Staats, 1999).

The desired unification is to be achieved by following the path taken by the more successful sciences that, although they began in chaotic disunity with a focus on producing new theories and findings (Staats, 1991, 1998, 1999), made the transition to working on the interrelationships among phenomena. When attention shifts to the interrelationship among phenomena, the focus of research becomes more directed, investigators become more collaborative and less concerned with discrediting the work of others (Staats, 1991). In due time, a comprehensive, organizing principle emerges. This accelerates consolidation, leading to a greater, more efficient accumulation and elaboration of knowledge and additional consistency within the field (Henriques, 2003).

The development of a unifying paradigm for psychology will be difficult but not impossible. Impeding progress to this desirable goal is the breadth of current psychology. The number of fields and subfields and sub-subfields is ever-growing. So too is the number of psychologists. When physics, considered to be a prototypical science, was in its preparadigmic stage, there were relatively few people involved in the field; therefore, it was comparatively easy for any one physicist to keep abreast of most new research developments and to attain a broad understanding of all aspects of the field. However, it would be impossible for any one person to master all that is psychology (Staats, 1991), which only makes the task of developing a unified theory that much harder (Henriques, 2003). In addition, the tendency of psychologists to perform correlational studies rather than experiments lends findings a subjective quality that hampers paradigmic development (Henriques, 2003).

These difficulties, although many in number, may be overcome with more focus on seeking causal connections through experimental research (Henriques, 2003). Unification will also be facilitated by training students of psychology in constructing theory, encouraging psychologists with different areas of focus to work together, and requiring continuing education in areas of psychology other than one's current area of expertise (Staats, 1991). Furthermore, common principles and redundancies in accepted theories should be studied, with an eye on finding underlying relationships among them (Staats, 1980, 1991).

However ardent some psychologists may be for unification, others may view that end as not necessary, desirable, or even possible. To gain perspective on the matter, we sent a survey to 50 psychologists we know. In selecting this convenience sample, we included those who identified themselves as psychologists yet represented diverse specialties of the discipline. Among the questions put were the following:

> "Most current introductory textbooks in psychology define it as the study (or science) of behavior and mental processes. Would you alter the definition in any way?"
> "What ought be the aims of psychology?"
> "Does psychology require a greater degree of unification if your goals for psychology are to be achieved?"
> "Do you believe psychology is becoming more unified?"
> "Ought psychology become more unified?"
> "Is a unified psychology possible?"

Of the 50 surveyed, 30 replied. Before summarizing their responses, two points need to be made. First, we make no claim that what follows represents anything more than our attempt to capture the beliefs about the unity of psychology of those sampled, to provide a snapshot of the opinions of a diverse group of psychologists. Second, at best, we have reported accurately what our respondents think and not what ought to be or what would be best for psychology and psychologists.

To the definition of psychology presented them as found in most introductory psychology texts, "the study of the science of behavior and mental processes," some respondents tacked on the equivalent of "and their relationship to society"; others added phrases such as "the treatment of behavioral dysfunction and the amelioration of the human condition through applications"; yet others included such terms as "emotions" and "neurological," "cultural," and "social/behavior." In effect, the definitions of psychology tendered denote a discipline of enormous range, importance, and diversity. With permission of the respondents, we cite two definitions illustrative of this conclusion. The first was provided by the social psychologist Vita Rabinowitz; the second by Ethel Tobach, a comparative psychologist.

> I might describe it the same way, as this is as good a definition as any, but this definition does not capture the significant applied research and clinical applications that are important. Much as I agree that psychology is a science, I think that the definition you cite exaggerates the consensus of the field. There is no single paradigm to this day. Instead, there are many competing perspectives that psychologist take: evolutionary,

social/cultural, psychoanalytic, neurosciences, etc., that are hard to reconcile. (Vita Rabinowitz)

Psychology is the study of the activities of organisms that subsume their evolutionary and developmental histories, their relationships with the environments in which they developed and were active throughout their life span, and the various systems of the individual organism, such as physiology, biochemistry (genes and hormones), neurology, and the integration of such knowledge with the development of practices and policies that aim to benefit the lives of those organisms. (Ethel Tobach)

Not surprisingly, the query about the appropriate goals of psychology drew answers echoing those given to the question about an apt definition of the field. Of the 25 who responded to this question, seven indicated that the primary goal of the field should be to enhance the understanding of human (and animal) functioning, behavior, or mental processes; six to increase life's quality, ease suffering, and help people (and animals) to lead happier lives; the rest advocated some mix of the two. In particular, the majority of respondents indicated that research into human behavior should inform the making of governmental policies.

An interesting pattern emerged from the replies offered to the set of questions about the unification of psychology. To say the very least, our respondents were ambivalent on the matter. All except one who answered this question (26 of 27) saw particular benefits to greater unification. Chief among the scientific gains foreseen were greater conceptual cross-fertilization, an increase in knowledge acquisition, and a better understanding of the interrelationships among constructs. Foremost among the professional advantages mentioned was enhanced political influence for the field as a whole.

Given that almost all of the psychologists surveyed saw benefits in unification, it is not surprising that many saw the fragmentation of the field as a liability. Loss of cross-fertilization of ideas or lack of communication was a concern for 12 of the 22 people who responded to this question. For example:

> "Overspecialization results in loss of perspective and lessens opportunities for benefiting from shared experiences."
> "It [fragmentation] results in less communication among related areas, which can retard progress."

One respondent indicated that fragmentation affected the perception of psychology as a science:

> On the negative side, fragmentation means that our discipline has a hard time convincing itself and others that it is a science and that it makes progress in its understanding of behavior and mental and emotional processes.

One respondent replied that fragmentation could lead to competition among psychological organizations for members, making such organizations economically unviable. Another suggested that psychology's institutional divisions make political influence more difficult to attain.

The prospect of psychology's unification clearly was not viewed as an unmitigated good by our respondents. Just as all but one saw benefits to unification, all but one indicated that it had associated drawbacks. Respondents worried that an attempt to unify the field would hamper the development of new areas of study and produce less specialization. Some saw unification in organizational terms, as "likely to lead to huge organizations" in which decision making and activity planning would become even more cumbersome. And just as many as those who identified specific problems in psychology's fragmentation found it advantageous. Pluses mentioned included, for example, that "Separate schools of thought can follow a stream of research and application more closely and clearly"; "Specialization may be a necessary route to gain greater knowledge"; and "Fragmentation leads to greater intellectual diversity and such diversity is in itself beneficial." Nonetheless, half of respondents indicated that overall, psychology would need to become more unified to achieve the aims that they envisioned for it:

"Psychology needs a core if it [is] to remain a viable discipline. There must be some common basis by which to identify psychologists beyond their degree"; "Unification is compelling and seductive. It characterizes the more mature 'paradigmatic' sciences like physics and chemistry, disciplines to which many in psychology aspire."

Despite their voiced preferences for greater unification, 22 of the respondents thought that as a discipline psychology was becoming increasingly diverse. Three others felt that psychology was, "paradoxically," becoming both more unified and diverse. For example, Vita Rabinowitz indicated that

> psychology . . . is more diverse in that it accommodates more and more different types of perspectives and peoples, attempts to describe more and more phenomena from the biological and chemical to the social and cultural. . . . On the other hand, we have many forces attempting to unify psychology. We are again in the era of major connectivist theories, for example, and evolutionary psychology attempts to explain much of human behavior.

Only one person saw little change in psychology. In her view, the field was becoming neither more diverse nor more unified.

In part, driving the belief that greater unity—if not unification—was desirable was the conviction that not only were some of its specialties becoming more and more distinct but some were actually moving away from psychology and toward greater affiliation with other disciplines. This trend was seen as most pronounced for psychology's "science"-oriented specialties with strong interdisciplinary ties. For example, one respondent felt that the neurosciences were more or less divorced from other areas of psychological study and that cognitive psychology was on the way out as well. Furthermore, several respondents noted a widening gap between the science- (e.g. neuroscience, experimental, biological psychology) and practice- (e.g. clinical, school) focused areas of the discipline. In all, 20 respondents reported particular areas in psychology were becoming increasingly separated from the rest of the field.

When attention shifted from the discipline as a whole onto its specialties, an equal number of psychologists believed certain areas in psychology were becoming more unified and others less. Those viewed as becoming more integrated were neuroscience with the cognitive–behavioral, clinical with neuroscience, clinical with developmental, and social with health psychology.

The respondents' opinions about whether a more complete unification of psychology was indeed possible were divided. Fifteen respondents indicated that unification was not possible, and nine said it was. (One respondent was undecided; others left the question blank.) Reasons given by the 15 included the belief that there never has been "one" psychology and the trend toward increasing specialization in the field. However, one's belief about unification's possibility did not necessarily reflect one's stance regarding its potential benefits. Although one respondent indicated that unification would simply be a "bad idea," another wrote, "It is theoretically possible, and even desirable, but I see it as a long way off." In fact, a number of respondents indicated unification ought be a goal of psychology. One respondent commented, "I do not think that you give up on searching for a paradigm that will be powerful and useful just because the paradigm has proved maddeningly elusive."

In regard to particular areas of psychology that would or would not benefit from increased unification, only three respondents indicated that there was no particular need for applied areas to draw more from research. Other respondents indicated that specific areas would benefit from greater coordination; they suggested memory, learning, and neuropsychology might be better combined with social aspects of psychology, for example.

One rough index of an issue's importance is its saliency. If the responses of the respondents are the guide and if the term *unification* connotes moving the discipline to a single paradigm, then unification of the discipline has a relatively low priority for most psychologists. Half of the survey respondents said that they saw no discernible efforts to unify different aspects of psychology in the current literature. Although the other half did note such efforts, they held varied opinions about what exactly unification meant. Some respondents saw efforts toward unification in particular areas, citing as examples the increasing "cognitivation" of social psychology and the forging of good working relationships between education and clinical psychology. Others referred to particular articles or researchers advocating for unity.

In summary, we believe it is fair to report that our respondents think that both psychology and they, themselves, would benefit if the discipline were more unified. The unity they seek is not a reconstitution of the discipline brought about by the adoption of a single defining paradigm, especially if doing so would require shedding many of psychology's diverse specialties and goals. Rather, the aims of our respondents are more modest. They would prefer greater educational and research effort be put into defining the communality among psychology's many specialties. All but one respondent believed that all undergraduate majors and graduate students in psychology (regardless of area of specialization) should master a core body of knowledge and skills. For psychology majors, required courses at the least would include introductory, history, research methods (including statistics), and experimental. (Although other courses were also deemed essential by some, none achieved consensus.)

The slate of core courses recommended for graduate students was quite similar to that for the undergraduates. Mentioned repeatedly were methodology, history of psychology, research, ethics, and understanding diverse populations. As one respondent stated, "All psychologists need a basic understanding of the core subdisciplines of psychology." Does this mean a return to the proseminar—a suggestion that goes in and out of favor?

The nearly unanimous view that both undergraduates and graduates each should have a common core of courses certainly speaks to the idea of unity through diversity and the recognition of psychology as one discipline albeit with a variety of subfields. No one suggested that psychology should fragment—quite the reverse, in fact.

Our respondents' view of whether unification should be addressed in teaching—and if so, how—was less clear. Although most respondents appeared to think unification could be dealt with in the classroom, there was little agreement about how this should be approached. Some respondents favored teaching "diverse aspects of psychology" and others "looking more at the whole picture and not focusing too much on the microcosms." Respondents also emphasized that greater investigative attention needs to be paid to determine the interrelationships among consensually agreed on constructs and less to unnecessarily proliferating the arrays of putative variables generated by undisciplined theory making. In summary, it is fair to say that the respondents feel the strain that is inherent in the width, breadth, and depth of psychology's commitments but have yet to experience panic as a result of it. The remedy sought, therefore, is ameliorative rather than radical.

The Roots of Psychology's Diversity

No consensus emerged among our respondents that the adoption of a core, singular, unifying paradigm for doing psychology would speed its work, would be desirable, or would be possible. Be that as it may, from time to time the longing for such a consistent and cohesive framework arises in the hearts of many thoughtful psychologists, most typically those associated with the "hard science" specialties of the discipline. Often it is instigated by the advance of a sister science. These psychologists note, with enormous envy, the impressive accomplishments of that science (the science most recently in the spotlight is biology) and wish the same success for psychology.

Although we are not in agreement that psychology's contributions pale in comparison to those of the hard sciences, we acknowledge that concerns about psychology's progress are not uncommon. They were raised, for example, by Wolfle (1963) more than four decades ago in his introductory comments to "Psychology: The History of a Science" (Koch, 1963), and, given our respondents' comments, are still relevant today.

> Psychology has not one sure sense of direction but several quite unsure directions. Growth is erratic, and there is much casting about for the most crucial problems and most powerful methods. These apparent differences between psychology and the older branches of science may result from the difficulty of developing a science of man. ... Or the differences may be an illusion resulting from the much closer view we have of the beginning struggles to develop a science of psychology than we now have of the beginning efforts in the older sciences.

> Certainly psychology has its problems, and they are not easy. Nevertheless, knowledge has grown rapidly in the short history of man's efforts to develop a science of behavior, and the time seems appropriate for a major effort to examine the progress that has been made in attempting to find a way, or ways, to the attainment of explanatory power that we like to think of as characteristic of science. (Wolfle, 1963, p. vii)

Furthermore, the intuition that psychology, more so than the physical and biological sciences, is characterized by fiat and fashion rather than an evolving clarity in theoretical exposition that allows for the subsumption of facts and the prediction or understanding of new results has been with us for a long time. To illustrate, we cite Koch (1963):

> As for the present interest in learning–perception relations, this admirable development, it must be recalled, occurred only after the field of perception itself had been all but legislated out of existence (at least in this country) for a period of roughly 30 years. Learning has

pre-empted perception during the hegemony of behaviorism and neo-behaviorism. (p. 10)

We leave it to the reader to decide if learning is now assimilated and better understood under the umbrella of cognition–perception.

The conclusion that for some reason the discipline, taken as a whole, has not produced a firm understanding about how to accumulate knowledge systematically is strengthened if one takes the effort to review how definitions of the field have changed over time. This is an especially forceful demonstration if one considers that at any given time the definition ascribed to it is a "projection back" rather than a portrayal of it in terms of the meaningful activity it was in the past (Gregory, 1987; Smith, 1988). Psychologists, for example, once talked about cognition, conation, and affection (Koch, 1963). Later on, in its last major effort at a unifying paradigm, psychology became the science of behavior. Inferred "mental states" were then relegated to the wastebasket of pseudoscience or to an unrealized future when they could unequivocally be operationalized. In fact, in historical perspective, cognitive science may be viewed as developing out of a reaction against behaviorism and its aversion to "inner states" (Baumgartner & Payr, 1995). Today, as vague as it may seem to some, we have as psychology's definition the "study (or science) of behavior and mental processes," and even this definition seemed too narrow for our respondents.

Various alternative explanations have been forwarded to account for the discipline's alleged lack of progress. These include, besides the complexity of the human condition, the breadth of psychology's purview and relative youth as a science, if not as a focus of inquiry, and its diversity. Although all of these factors play a role in making psychology a challenging area of intellectual endeavor, it is the last of these to which we shall attend.

To a degree, that which constitutes psychology is largely arbitrary and a function of historical accident. The discipline is, as Campbell suggested, a "hodge podge of sensitive subjective biography, of brain operations, of school achievement testing, of factor analysis, of Markov process mathematics, of schizophrenic families, of laboratory experiments on group structure in which persons are anonymous" (Campbell, 1969, p. 33). Psychology was not at its founding, and is not today, however, uniquely characterized by its diversity of context and method. These traits have been and remain common to all of the so-called social or human sciences—for example, in sociology, history, political science, and so forth (Campbell, 1969, p. 332)— and at one stage in their development, also characterized the physical and biological sciences. For the physical and biological sciences, this seems to be the case no longer, or if it is still so, it is to a considerably lesser magnitude than for the social sciences. Apparently what has occurred, for example, in biology (and according to some of our respondents in some of the areas of psychology related to it or another of the "hard" sciences), is a winnowing that removed from considerations by the discipline ideas and constructions that were not amenable to test by the evolving truth-seeking procedures of the field, truth-seeking methods that effectively and accurately assessed investigative results and their explanations.

Although some of the sifting necessary to reduce the proliferation of ambiguous indexes, constructs, and theories would occur in psychology if more attention were paid to such efforts as mapping the variable constellations that defined its many fields and subareas, seeking "bridging laws" that related each to each, and taking care to reduce unwanted redundancy among variables, we have a suspicion that even if these useful tactics were generally adopted and fiercely pursued, that the psychology that emerged thereafter would not resemble Staat's (1991, 1998, 1999) vision of a paradigmatically unified science. We doubt that such steps in themselves would select from the discipline's diverse fields that which is valuable and integrate that material appropriately and meaningfully into some future comprehensive theory.

Psychology as it is conceived today, we believe, cannot be embraced by a unifying paradigm identical to that of the natural and biological sciences. This is because psychology differs from these sciences in fundamental ways and must continue to do so. Although certain areas of psychology bear close relationship to these sciences, others do not. If those that do not were stripped away, a unifying paradigm might be found for the remaining. But, we believe, and our respondents concur, that in the long run, psychology would be poorer for the removal. It is in psychology's underlying diversity that its strength, essence, and enchantment lie.

Of all of the sciences, psychology lies closest, according to Gordon Allport (1960), to the turbulent convergence of the four winds of the intellectual heavens: the natural sciences, the biological sciences, the social sciences, and the humanities. Each presses on psychology and, at any given time, has a greater or lesser influence on the direction and course of its development.

> And I suppose no younger sister ever had as an acute an inferiority complex as psychology has in relation to her well-groomed and socially correct elder sister [physics] . . . It's of course, particularly in the study of sensation that the physical sciences dominate psychology. . . .
>
> From the *biological sciences* also came high standards and exacting methods of research, as well as the evolutionary and organismal points of view without which psychology would still be scholastic in character. . . .
>
> In many quarters . . . [biology has] threatened to push every vestige of humanism out, leaving psychology with a plague of rats.

Social science is causing a tornado on its own. It refuses to blend amicably with natural and biological science, but claims mind pretty much as its own province for study. Mind, they insist, takes its form almost wholly in response to cultural demands.

The last wind that blows into our storm center is gentler and less voracious. . . . It is the wind of humanism. After all is said and done, it is philosophy and literature . . . that fostered psychology throughout the ages. (Allport, 1960, p. 45)

Because it is so much a product of each of these intellectual forces, we believe that if it is to be successful, psychology must take into account the aims, strengths, and limitations that are inherent in the methods of each. It must take the best from each and use the resulting synthesis to its own ends.

In a lecture to the Harvard physics department, according to Herschbach (1996), the noted physicist I. I. Rabi lamented,

How can we hope to obtain wisdom, the wisdom which is meaningful in our own time. . . . We certainly cannot attain it as long as the two great branches of human knowledge, the sciences and the humanities, remain separate and even warring disciplines. . . .

Our problem is to blend these two traditions. . . . The greatest difficulty which stands in the way . . . [is] communication. (Rabi, 1996; also cited in Herschbach, 1996, p. 24)

Rabi later had occasion to discuss these thoughts with C. P. Snow. Snow developed them in his influential and quite popular *Two Cultures and the Scientific Revolution* (1962). In it, Snow argued that the sciences, on one hand, and the humanities, on the other, had become two distinct and mutually unintelligible cultures. He attributed this largely to a lack of scientific training and knowledge in those interested in and educated in the humanities. Besides considering the two culture arguments a gross simplification of the actual state of affairs, Isaiah Berlin (e.g., 1997, 1998), a historian of ideas, argued cogently that Snow had missed a deeper point: The "estrangement" of the sciences and humanities was a consequence of their somewhat differing interests and the differing styles of inquiry with which they addressed them. He saw the separation of the two as emblematic of the historical dialectic between the conviction that the "world" was a single system that, in principle, could be understood rationally and the reaction to that very idea.

In the 19th century, the contention between these two antagonistic world views, the former embodied in the Enlightenment and the latter in the Counter-Enlightenment, gave birth to the division between the *Naturwissenschaften* and the *Geisteswissenschaften*, the natural sciences and the humanities. For the natural sciences, two assumptions are fundamental:

a. Every genuine question has one true answer and one only: all others being false. Unless this is so, the question cannot be a real question—there is a confusion in it somewhere. . . .

b. The method which leads to correct solutions is rational in character and is, in essence if not in detailed application, identical in all fields. These solutions, whether or not they are discussed, are true universally, eternally, and immutably: true for all times, places, and men: as in the old definition of natural law, they are quod ubique, quod semper, quodab omnibus creditum est. (Berlin, 1998, pp. 326–327)

To the humanities, however, these presuppositions are viewed as the framework for a Procrusteau Bed, more likely to injure than fit its body of interests. (Today, far from being just the covering name given to identity politics—the politics of race, gender, sexual preference, and class [Goodheart, 1997]—"postmodernism" represents the Counter-Enlightenment pole of that ancient dialectic.) And, like it or not, psychology possesses aspects of both the natural sciences and the humanities. If it is to be true to its aims, we believe psychology must develop and adopt a working synthesis of the methods of each. Whether it will be able to do so successfully remains to be seen.

Consilience

The natural and biological sciences of today are the living embodiments of the Enlightenment's hopes. Perhaps the most visible spokesperson today of the possibility of using an objective, empirical, inductive approach to gain a true account of everything or almost everything is the biologist Edmund O. Wilson. His word for the method by which this is to be accomplished is *consilience:*

The central idea of the consilience world view is that all tangible phenomena, from the birth of the stars to the working of social institutions, are based on material processes that are ultimately reducible however long and tortuous the sequence, to the laws of physics. . . . The strategy [of reductionism] that works best in these enterprises is the construction of coherent cause-and-effect explanations across levels of organization. . . . No compelling reason has ever been offered why the same strategy should not work to link the natural sciences with the social sciences and humanities. The difference between the two is in the magnitude of the problem, not the principles needed for its solution.

To dissect a phenomenon into its elements . . . is consilience by reduction. To reconstruct it, and especially to predict with knowledge gained by reduction how nature assembled it in the first place, is consilience by synthesis. That is the two-step procedure by which natural scientists generally work, top down across two or three levels of organization at a time by analysis, the bottom up across the same level by synthesis. (Wilson, 1998, pp. 73–74)

Although reductionism has proved to be a powerful and useful treatment, it fails as a panacea even if its use is confined to the *Naturwissenschaften*. Its shortcomings are both logical and empirical, and, to his credit, Wilson (1998) recognized that as he envisioned it, consilience, in its strongest form, may be flawed at worst and oversimplified at best.

What are the shortcomings of consilience? Stephen J. Gould sees them as twofold. He has written that he does not

> believe that reductionism can come even close to full success as a style of explanation for levels of complexity (including several aspects of evolutionary biology, and proceeding "upward" in intricacy toward cognitive and social systems of ever greater integration and interaction) for two basic reasons that allow these subjects to remain fully within the element of factual and knowable science, but that require additional styles of explanation for their resolution. . . . First, emergence, or the entry of novel explanatory rules in complex systems, laws arising from "nonlinear" or "nonadditive" interactions among constituent parts that therefore, in principle, cannot be discovered from the two properties of the parts considered separately (their status in the "basic" sciences that provide the fundamental principles of explanation in classically reductionistic models). Second, contingency, or the growing importance of unique historical "accidents" that cannot, in principle, be predicted, but that remain fully accessible to factual explanations after their occurrence. The role of contingency as a component of explanation increase in the same sciences of complexity that also become more and more inaccessible to reductionism for the first reason of emergent principles. (Gould, 2003, pp. 201–202)

The point is that if a coherent, comprehensive discipline of psychology is to be achieved, much more than the reductionism or its correctives developed for the hard sciences will be required. If psychology is to fulfill its ends, the discipline will have to acknowledge its roots in the humanities and, in addition, to the methods of the physical and biological sciences, apply those truth-finding techniques that spring from that alternate, although no less important Western intellectual tradition, one that recognized, in contrast to that of the "objectivity" and "universality" of the Modern Enlightenment that

> there existed a world of knowledge beyond natural science. Of the most obviously man-made constructions—works of art, political schemes, legal systems, and indeed all rule-determined disciplines—which men could know from within. . . . [It] was the story of human activities, of what men did and thought and suffered, of what they strove for, aimed

at, accepted, rejected, conceived, imagined, of what their feelings were directed at. It was concerned, therefore, with motives, purposes, hopes, fears, loves and hatreds, jealousies, ambitions, outlooks and visions of reality; with the ways of seeing, and ways of acting and creating, of individuals and groups. These activities we knew directly, because we were involved in them as actors, not spectators. There was a sense, therefore, in which we knew more about ourselves than we knew about the external world; when we studied, let us say, Roman law, or Roman institutions, we were not contemplating objects in nature, of whose purposes, or whether they had any, we could know nothing. We had to ask ourselves what these Romans were at, what they strove to do, how they lived and thought, what kind of relationship with other men they were anxious to promote or frustrate. We could not ask this about natural objects. . . . There was, therefore, a clear sense in which our knowledge was superior, at least in kind, about intentional behavior. . . . What was opaque to us when we contemplated the external world was, if not wholly transparent, yet sure far more so when we contemplated ourselves. It was therefore a perverse kind of self-denial to apply the rules and laws of physics or the other natural sciences to the world of mind and will and feeling; for by doing this we would be gratuitously debarring ourselves from much that we could know. (Berlin, 1998, pp. 342–343)

To understand this world instead of removing ourselves from it, we must project ourselves into it, imagine it, and empathize with it.

The recognition of a given piece of behavior as being part and parcel of a pattern of activity which we can follow, remember or imagine, and which we can describe in terms of the general laws which cannot possibly all be rendered explicit (still less organized into a system), but without which the texture of normal human life—social or personal— is not conceivable. We may make mistakes, be shallow, unobservant, naïve, etc. not allow, allow for unconscious motives or unintended consequences, or chance. We may project present into past or assume incorrectly our rules apply to other societies. All such explanations cannot be rejected in toto without cutting ground from beneath our feet, the context in which we think.

When I understand a sentence which someone utters, my claim to know what he means is not, as a rule, based on an indirectly reached conclusion that the statistical probability is that the noises he emits are, in fact, related and expressive in the way that I take them to be— a conclusion described from a comparison of the sound he utters with a great many other sounds that a great many other beings have uttered in corresponding situations in the past. . . . Yet we do not for this reason regard such claims to understanding as being less rational than scientific convictions, still less as being arbitrary. (Berlin, 1979, pp. 128–129)

Goffman (1983) made the point this way:

> To utter something and to not disconfirm that we are sane requires that our saying be heard to draw approximately on one array of presuppositions—that sustained by our hearers and avoid being heard to make others—those which are not, although they may be by persons not present. Responding to another's words, we must find a phrasing that answers not merely to the other's words but to the other's mind—so that the other can draw both from the local scene and from the distal, wider worlds, of her or his experience. (Goffman, 1983, p. 48)

A Blended Epistemology

Just as the natural sciences have, the humanities have developed characteristic practices for producing systematic knowledge. The set of techniques used to provide an epistemology for the *Geisteswissenschaften* (Grondin, 2003) is termed *hermeneutics*. Hermeneutics arose out of philology and Homeric and Biblical studies (Campbell, 1988). If observation is the key to how the natural sciences make discoveries (Feynman, 1998), *verstehen* and empathy serve that purpose for the humanities.

> A scholar is deciphering an archaic text. On first reading he gets only fragmentary hunches, which he forces into a guess at the overall direction of the message. Using this, he goes over it again, decoding a bit more, deciding on plausible translations of a few words he has never encountered before. He repeats this hermeneutic cycle or spiral again and again, revising past guesses and making new ones for previously unattempted sections. If he is being successful and has extensive enough texts to properly prove his translation hypotheses, he arrives at such a remarkable confidence that he can in places decide that the ancient scribe made a clerical error, and that he, the modern, knows better what that ancient intended than what the ancient's written text records. I believe such things happen, and often validly so. It well illustrates this holistic dependence on fallible elements, since any part of the text could have been a clerical error. (Campbell, 1988, p. 478)

The most profound and, indeed, optimistic American proponent of the importance of hermeneutics to the epistemology of science in general and psychology in particular was Donald T. Campbell. We consider him optimistic because he rejected the "currently fashionable hermeneutic nihilism, in which validity of interpretation is rejected as a goal" (Campbell, 1988, p. 505) and saw that which he termed "validity-seeking hermeneutics" as combining elements from the methodologies of the natural sciences and the humanities into an effective strategy for increasing and perfecting psychological knowledge (Campbell, 1988).

Campbell began to explore the epistemological potential of validity-seeking hermeneutics when he became convinced that the rejection of logical positivism by philosophers of science required a general rethinking of the theory of science with an increased focus on methodological concerns.

> Twenty years ago, logical positivism dominated the philosophy of science, and through concepts like operational definition, dominated our thoughts about research methods. Today the tide has completely turned among the theorists of science in philosophy, sociology, and elsewhere.
> Logical positivism is almost universally rejected. This rejection . . . has left our theory of science in disarray. Under some interpretations it has undermined our determination to be scientific and our faith that validity and truth are natural and reasonable goals, what we should have learned instead was that logical positivism was a gross misreading of the method of the already successful sciences. Logical positivism was wrong in rejecting casual processes imputed to unobserved variables. Logical positivism failed to recognize that even at its best, experimental research is equivocal and ambiguous in relation both to the real physical process involved and to scientific theory, and that attention to this equivocally calls for the use of multiple methods, more of them definitional triangulating as causal processes that are imperfectly exemplified in our experimental treatments and measurement process. Properly interpreted, the dethronement of logical positivism should have led to an increase in methodological concern rather than its abandonment. (Campbell, 1988, p. 316)

In confronting the challenge of finding a viable substitute for positivism, Campbell became impressed by what appeared to him to be the convergence of postpositivistic methodological thinking from the hard science camp on the one hand and the central themes in the hermeneutic tradition on the other (to say nothing of his own epistemological predispositions). He concluded that the evolving combination of the two—postpositivist natural science and hermeneutic epistemologies—held promise for resolving many of the procedural difficulties that seemed to him to have inhibited psychology's overall development. He saw that if a unifying paradigm for psychology were indeed possible, one that would encompass appropriately psychology's diversity, it would necessarily be the outcomes of the emerging synthesis of the two traditions—that of the *Naturwissenschaften* and *Geistenwissenschaften*.

It is well beyond this chapter's scope to detail the validity-seeking hermeneutic principles to which Campbell subscribed, although it might be useful to name them. Beyond the hermeneutic circle already mentioned, he offered the following: (a) omnifallibust trust; (b) pattern matching; (c) increasing correspondence with increasing scope; (d) partial proximal revision; (e) fallibilist privileging of observation and core; (f) principle of charity; and (g) paradigm, linguistic, and cultural solipsism. Extended definitions of these terms may be found in Campbell (1991).

Campbell himself had no doubt that whenever individuals committed to an intellectual discipline engaged in the honest, communal, truth-seeking disputation whose goal was increasing its base of knowledge, progress resulted. We look forward with anticipation, therefore, to the next phase of the continuing debate about the proper study of psychology and to the positive influence that informed constructive argumentation will exert on the disciplines evolving epistemology.

CONCLUSION

By almost every conceivable standard, psychology is an extraordinarily successful discipline. It plays an important role in our intellectual life. Those formally trained in it apply its results in settings that range from the clinic to the school, from the design studio to the Fortune 500 company. Furthermore, psychology's influence is growing and there is no sign that this growth will slow soon. Yet psychology's very success has produced interdisciplinary strain. One indication that this is so is the suggestion that psychology, if it is to make the contribution of which it is capable, requires reformation. The course of treatment suggested is unification. Now unification has many connotations: Some suggest evolutionary change, others, structural revolution. Both our respondents and we recognize not only the utility but the desirability of psychology having greater unity. Both our respondents and we would, for example, like to see greater integration achieved among psychology's specialties, more attention paid to the interrelationship between and among its constructs, indexes, and theories, and greater harmony attained between those who disseminate its findings and those who produce them. We believe these ends can be accomplished without radically changing the structure of the discipline.

The call for a unifying paradigm for psychology has revolutionary implications. If its intent is to further psychology's adoption of the methodological practices of the natural and biological sciences, then we are against it. There is no doubt in our minds that such a course of action will prove unwise. Its cost will be the dismemberment of psychology. Whatever the gain, it will be exceeded by the loss of a great deal that is central to psychology and psychologists. In addition, we believe that any attempt by psychology to emulate the past and dated epistemology of the natural sciences is ill-conceived. We are convinced that psychology's diverse specialties contain, in different proportion, elements of the natural sciences and the humanities. If it is indeed possible to unify psychology under the umbrella of a single paradigm, that paradigm must be a synthesis of these two great streams of the western intellectual tradition.

REFERENCES

Allport, G. W. (1960). *Personality and social encounter*. Boston: Beacon Press.

Baumgartner, P., & Payr, S. (Eds.). (1995). *Speaking minds*. Princeton, NJ: Princeton University Press.

Berlin, I. (1979). *Concepts and categories: Philosophical essay by Isaiah Berlin*. New York: Viking.

Berlin, I. (1997). *The sense of reality: Studies in the ideas and their history*. New York: Farrar, Strauss & Giroux.

Berlin, I. (1998). *The proper study of mankind: An anthology of essays* (H. Hardy & R. Hausheer, Eds.). New York: Farrar, Straus, & Giroux.

Campbell, D. T. (1969). Ethnocentrism of disciplines and the fish-scale model of omniscience. In M. Sherif & C. W. Sherif (Eds.), *Interdisciplinary relationships in the social sciences* (pp. 328–348). Chicago: Aldine.

Campbell, D. T. (1988). *Methodology and epistemology for social sciences: Selected papers* (E. Samuel Overman, Ed.). Chicago: University of Chicago.

Campbell, D. T. (1991). *Coherent empiricism hermeneutics and the commensurability of paradigms*. Unpublished manuscript.

Eysenck, H. J. (1997). Personality and experimental psychology: The unification of psychology and the possibility of a paradigm. *Journal of Personality and Social Psychology, 73*, 1224–1237.

Feynman, R. P. (1998). *The meaning of it all*. Reading, MA: Perseus.

Goffman, I. (1983). Felicity's condition. *American Journal of Sociology, 81*, 1–53.

Goodheart, E. (1997). Reflection on the culture wars. *Daedelus, 126*, 153–175.

Gould, S. J. (2003). *The hedgehog, the fox, and the magister's pox: Mending the gap between science and the humanities*. New York: Harmony.

Gregory, R. L. (1987). *The Oxford companion to mind*. Oxford, England: Oxford University Press.

Grondin, J. (2003). *Hans-Georg Gadamer*. New Haven, CT: Yale University Press.

Henriques, G. (2003). The tree of knowledge system and the theoretical unification of psychology. *Review of General Psychology, 7*(2), 150–182.

Herschbach, D. R. (1996). Imaginary gardens with real toads. The flight from science and reason. *Annals of the New York Academy of Sciences, 775*, 11–30.

Koch, S. (1963). Psychology: A study of a science. In S. Koch (Ed.), *Investigations of man as socius* (Vol. 6, pp. 1–29). New York: McGraw-Hill.

Rabi, I. I. (1996). Lecture to students in Harvard's physics department. Cited in D. R. Herschbach, Imaginary gardens with real toads. The flight from science and reason. *Annals of the New York Academy of Sciences, 775*, 11–30.

Smith, R. (1988). Does the history of psychology have a subject? *History of the Human Sciences, 1*, 147–177.

Snow, C. P. (1962). *Two cultures and the scientific revolution*. New York: Cambridge University Press.

Staats, A. W. (1991). Unified positivism and unification psychology. *American Psychologist, 46*, 899–912.

Staats, A. W. (1998). Unifying psychology: A scientific or non-scientific task? *Journal of Theoretical and Philosophical Psychology, 18*, 70–79.

Staats, A. W. (1999). Unifying psychology requires new infrastructure, theory, method, and research agenda. *Review of General Psychology, 3*(1), 3–13.

Wilson, E. O. (1998). *Consilience*. New York: Knopf

Wolfle, D. (1963) Preface. In S. Koch (Ed.), *Psychology: A study of a science*. Vol. 6 *Investigations of man as socius: Their place in psychology and the social sciences* (pp. vii–ix). New York: McGraw-Hill.

3

CASE-BASED STUDIES AS A SOURCE OF UNITY IN APPLIED PSYCHOLOGY

DANIEL B. FISHMAN AND STANLEY B. MESSER

To unify or not to unify applied psychology: That is the question. In this chapter we review pendulum swings in the historical efforts to answer this question, from a comprehensive, positivist, "top-down," deductive *yes* between the 1930s and the early 1960s to a postmodern *no* since then and until recently. We then present a rationale and proposal for a limited, "bottom-up," inductive *yes*, using a case-based paradigm that integrates both positivist and postmodern themes and components. We call this paradigm pragmatic psychology and its specific use of case studies the pragmatic case study method (PCS method), because it calls for the creation of peer-reviewed journal–databases of pragmatic case studies. To illustrate the general potential of the PCS method, we begin with a specific psychotherapy case, which provides the reader with a concrete entrée into the PCS method.[1]

---

[1]Note that the presentation of Mrs. B.'s case is not meant as a model case write-up of the kind that we have in mind for the new journal, *Pragmatic Case Studies in Psychotherapy*, which is described later in the chapter. Unlike the description of Mrs. B., which is designed to illustrate a particular point about the simultaneous use of multiple theoretical perspectives, the cases in the journal will be written up much more systematically and in depth. This is to enhance their level of rigor and to facilitate multidimensional comparison with other cases. To accomplish these goals, the case write-up includes an analysis in terms of Peterson's Disciplined Inquiry categories, described later in the chapter, and standardized, quantitative measures documenting assessment and outcome.

We then turn to the broader historical and epistemological arguments for the unifying nature of the PCS method and its application to the psychotherapy arena. Finally, we review three general approaches that have been in vogue over the past three decades to integrate and unify the disparate field of psychotherapy, and we suggest ways in which the PCS method can enhance these efforts at unification.

THE CASE OF MRS. B.

We now turn to the case of Mrs. B. to illustrate the potential of the PCS method for unifying across different theories in applied psychology. Our starting with a case embodies a theme of this chapter: An effective way to facilitate unifying processes in applied psychology is to ground the discussion of theory in qualitative "thick descriptions" of real cases.

Framework for Analyzing the Case: Using Multiple Theories Simultaneously as Pragmatic Tools

Sternberg, Grigorenko, and Kalmar (2001) argued that unification in basic research can be enhanced by creating a psychology that is phenomenon-oriented rather than theory-based—that is multi- rather than monoparadigmatic and multi- rather than monomethod. This vision in the basic research realm parallels the PCS method in the applied research realm. A focus on the phenomenon of study is equivalent to a focus on the actual case in practice, rather than on a theory of psychotherapy per se. In addition, Sternberg et al.'s (2001) advocacy of the coordinated and interlinked use of multiple methods and paradigms is parallel to the PCS method's unifying view of theories and methods as tools whose coordinated working together can be complementary. They can enhance the effectiveness of applied psychological interventions such as psychotherapy rather than act as competitors for discerning the single, true theory and a single, true method.

These ideas are illustrated in the case of Mrs. B., which highlights the capacity of the case study method to facilitate a multiparadigmatic approach in the effort to bring some degree of unity to psychotherapy. The example shows how an individual case can embrace contrasting conceptual perspectives in such a way as to improve on what could be achieved by any of these conceptualizations alone. In other words, the case demonstrates the value added by the four "visions of reality" (described later) working together. (For an expanded write-up of the case of Mrs. B. and the visions, see Messer, 2000; Messer & Woolfolk, 1998.)

The Case

Mrs. B. is a 45-year-old married, Jewish woman who has been feeling poorly for some time. For the past two months, she has experienced frequent crying spells, a lack of interest in people and activities, and a wish to run away from it all. She acknowledged some suicidal ideation but has no plan of action or history of suicide attempts. She failed to meet the criteria for major depressive disorder, but rather was diagnosed as depressive disorder, not otherwise specified (American Psychiatric Association, 1994, p. 311).

When asked what had happened two months ago, Mrs. B. responded that she had learned from her 16-year-old daughter that she had been sexually molested over a two-year period by her older brother when they were younger. Although her daughter acknowledges feeling depressed, she has not been willing to say more about what occurred and has recently started seeing a therapist at her mother's urging. Mrs. B. says she both wants to know and does not want to know what happened. She feels that she cannot tell her husband about it and is reluctant to confront her son for fear that revealing this information will "destroy the family." However, she finds herself having antagonistic feelings toward her son that are beginning to "leak out." Mrs. B. has tried to come to grips with the revelation about her children, but finds herself unable to do so, complaining that she was "falling fast and would soon explode." Over the past six months, she has taken several kinds of antidepressants that did not help her. Two weeks previously she started on a course of Prozac.

A significant background stressor, which has contributed in an important way to her feeling poorly, is her medical condition. She suffers constant, intractable pain from lupus, arthritis, and collagen vascular disorder; has high blood pressure; and is fearful that her life will be shortened by these ailments ("Lupus is like a slow cancer that will eventually attack my organs"). Walking is painful for her and she is unable to climb a flight of stairs. What worries her is that she will end up in a wheelchair. In addition, she had a breast removed five years ago when it was discovered that she had cancer, and received chemotherapy for a period of time. She was told that she has a genetic marker for cancer. One of the side effects of the several medications that she takes has been a weight gain of 50 pounds that very much distresses her. Not surprisingly, she worries about dying, wonders if there is a God, and "what comes next, after you die?"

Another ongoing stressor is that her husband lost his job a year ago and has not been able to find regular employment. He has started his own business, which is seasonal, and it is not yet financially solvent. In addition to working full-time in an administrative position in a large company, Mrs. B. tries to help her husband run his business.

The client describes her husband as a quiet, decent man, much like her deceased father, who lacks self-confidence and is both self-critical and very critical of others. He is passive, not a go-getter like her, she says, and he cannot handle too much at once. He tends to minimize her medical problems, which leaves her feeling that she has to face them alone. She would like him to be more affectionate to her and to be more helpful around the house, especially given her physical difficulties. She does most of the household chores herself—cooking, cleaning, handling bills—and rarely asks for help because she does not want to provoke arguments and risk her marriage coming to an end. It is likely that her husband is depressed, she says, and he is also taking Prozac.

Mrs. B. was married once before and divorced about 15 years ago. She describes her first marriage as physically and emotionally abusive in which she was hit and pushed around a great deal. Her two children are from that marriage. Her son is married and her daughter is in high school, but she is not performing well. Mrs. B. commented that she feels like she is a mother to everyone but gets nothing for herself. She feels guilty if she is not making others happy, yet is frustrated because she does not get to do what she wants to do. She wonders if she is trying to make up for her long-standing feeling of not being good enough.

Mrs. B.'s father died 10 years ago when he was 60 and she was 35. They had a close relationship and she still misses him. Her mother tries to be helpful to her but "babies me too much." In this vein, her mother lets her know that the proper role of a wife and mother is to cook, clean, and otherwise attend to all the physical and emotional needs of her family. When she was growing up, her mother was very strict with, and critical of, her.

Mrs. B. is well regarded at work, seems to take pleasure in the challenges there, and is striving to advance herself by taking workshops in her area of expertise. She tends to miss some days at work because of her medical condition, but is able to take work home. She is engaging to be with and, despite her many problems, conveys a degree of strength and perseverance under adverse circumstances. She has hobbies in the artistic realm that also give her pleasure.

Case Analysis

There are a variety of perspectives that can be used to conceptualize the clinical facts of the Mrs. B. case. In the discussion that follows, we have chosen four "visions of reality" for the analysis.

Visions of Reality in the Case of Mrs. B.

The visions of reality refer to the tragic, comic, romantic, and ironic genres of literature that have been elaborated on most extensively by the literary critic Northrop Frye (1957) and applied to psychoanalysis by Roy Schafer (1976). For a fuller exposition of the visions and how they apply to different forms of therapy, such as behavioral, humanistic, and psychoanalytic, see Messer and Winokur (1984) and Messer and Woolfolk (1998).

The Tragic Vision

In this section we try to imagine how the visions of reality might influence the angle of regard of the therapist at different points along the way in Mrs. B.'s therapy. In terms of content, the tragic vision would highlight the irreversible features of Mrs. B.'s life condition. She has reared her children and can undo little of whatever damage has accrued from the sexual contact between them. She must struggle with the attendant guilt of not having noticed, or not wanting to notice, what was happening at the time and in what way she may have been to blame. She has no easy choice facing her, whether it is to let sleeping dogs lie or to confront her children with their deeds. To do the former is to allow the wounds to fester and possibly to spoil her relationship with her son. To do the latter is to risk a permanent rupture among several members of her family. From the tragic perspective, the piper must be paid.

Mrs. B.'s medical condition is chronic and is slated to worsen. One cannot wish this away, in the spirit of the romantic vision, or avoid the daily reminders of her condition evidenced in her pain and difficulty walking. Her life possibilities are no longer what they once were—that is, she may have to accept that she will not get the college degree she wanted, or rise to greater heights in her company, simply because her physical condition might not allow it.

From the point of view of process and technique, the tragic view calls for exploration, reflection, and contemplation, which is most typical of psychoanalytic and humanistic approaches. The therapist participates in the client's problems in a manner similar to the audience's participation with the hero in a tragic drama. Just as the audience responds with pity and terror based on an identification with the hero's plight, the therapist responds empathically to the client based on resonance with similar tragic themes or echoes of them in his or her own life. The therapist also recognizes the ubiquity and universal nature of the kinds of conflict, anxieties, and suffering that the client faces. Understanding and treating them within the tragic vision call for an introspective and subjective stance with a thorough-going internal focus. Both the therapist and Mrs. B. come to realize, within the tragic view, that the best she can do is come to accept her fate with a certain degree of equanimity—a calm acceptance with a modicum of despair.

The tragic view, in isolation from the leavening provided by the other visions of reality, can lead to an overly gloomy and pessimistic therapeutic stance. The danger is in subtly encouraging the client to wallow in her angst, leading to passivity that would allow opportunities for action to pass her by. Some of this leavening comes from the therapist keeping in mind the comic vision.

The Comic Vision

As in comic drama, one might view the content of Mrs. B.'s problems as situational obstacles to be overcome through direct action. The problems can be framed as maladaptive interpersonal interactions among her and her children and between her and her husband, which are potentially ameliorable. Similarly, her husband's employment and business woes can be approached in a problem-solving mode that could improve Mrs. B.'s mood and reduce her anxiety. Ways can be proposed to improve her physical condition as well.

With respect to technique, within the comic vision one would approach Mrs. B. with a sense of optimism and can-do. True, she is depressed and life is not easy for her, but mental health practitioners have available tools and techniques to make things better. The client's depression can be alleviated with the appropriate medication, which will at least lift her mood, and/or she can be administered an empirically supported treatment for depression such as cognitive or interpersonal therapy (Task Force, 1995). Her distorted beliefs and maladaptive interpersonal relations may be improved in this way. Perhaps certain behavioral stress-reduction techniques, appropriate diet, and an exercise regimen would also help control her condition, albeit not cure it.

Regarding the relationship to her husband, she can be taught assertiveness training to get more of her own needs met and/or communication skills to improve their marriage. In this way a reconciliation between our "hero" and her "antagonist" could come about. With respect to her children, perhaps the situation can be cognitively reframed as their experimenting with sex to prepare themselves for adult life (as is accepted in some cultures), thus alleviating or eliminating her guilt.

The limitations or danger in this approach is "in the assumption that the therapist knows best and that the client merely has to follow advice in order to lead a satisfying life" (Andrews, 1989, p. 808), which can remove too much responsibility from clients for charting their own course and destiny. The comic vision can also induce expectations for cure in the client that are unrealistic, leading to disappointment.

The Romantic Vision

Within the romantic vision, the creative, fulfilling, and adventurous aspects of life are emphasized, even if there are temporary setbacks. In Mrs. B.'s case, she has artistic interests that can be capitalized on to help her live a more satisfying life. Regarding the process of therapy, Mrs. B. can be helped to strive to fulfill her potential in the work sphere and to develop her artistic talents as expressions of her true self. Her inner life of fantasies and daydreams can be explored with the view of encouraging her to see herself as a complex, striving individual who is not defined solely by her illnesses or her current life condition. She can be helped to live more in the moment than in the past. In general, the therapist, acting within the romantic tradition, holds an attitude of curiosity and openness to unexpected developments in the client, characteristic of the humanistic therapy tradition.

The danger in a one-sided emphasis on the romantic vision is of overplaying the creative possibilities and ignoring the client's and life's realistic limitations. Clearly, not all fantasies can be realized nor all aspirations fulfilled.

The Ironic Vision

This vision provides a corrective to the romantic vision in particular. The process or technique of therapy within the ironic vision calls for the therapist to be skeptical of all he or she sees and hears from the client. It encourages a questioning, challenging, even confronting attitude toward what the client says and does. The ironic vision also predisposes the therapist to keep the three visions in balance. Things may not be as bad as they seem for Mrs. B., but they are not infinitely malleable. One should not be too readily persuaded to side with Mrs. B.'s position or with that of her husband, her children, or her boss. What might seem at first blush like a clear case of fate conspiring against Mrs. B. may turn out to be her bringing things on herself—for example, by doing too much for others, by not standing her ground, and even by not attending to her illnesses in an optimal way. Might she have chosen accomplices to play out her cyclical maladaptive pattern?

Within the ironic vision, nothing should be taken at face value or for granted. The liability of the ironic stance is that its unremitting skepticism and confrontation can verge on hostility and lead to an intensification of the client's self-criticism (Andrews, 1989) and to accusatory interpretations (Wile, 1984).

Orchestrating the Visions

As we have suggested, the application of each life vision to therapy has its plus side and its minus side. What is the pragmatic value of taking all four visions into account? By being aware of the four visions and keeping them in mind simultaneously, the therapist does not allow the therapy to tilt too much toward the implications of one to the exclusion of the others. To do so might well turn out to be detrimental to the client. By having several perspectives available at the same time, the therapist can keep the treatment in proper balance.

Another reason to have all four visions at hand is that it expands the therapist's repertoire of responses, much as having a variety of tools provides flexibility of response for the craftsperson. One can then select those therapeutic tools (procedures, strategies, and so forth) that are tailored to the problem needing solution. After all, different visions are likely to be more or less apt at different points in therapy. For example, at a time when Mrs. B. was demoralized and depressed, one would not want to be confrontational, as might be called for within an ironic mode. Rather, taking action within the comic mode was considered more appropriate, such as encouraging her to be socially engaged rather than following her inclinations to withdraw; challenging her ruminative negative self-thoughts about her disabilities; and/or reminding her of her strengths. At other times, however, it might be therapeutic for her to be able to bemoan her fate and her failings as a mother and work toward an acceptance of herself and her life circumstances, as encompassed by the tragic vision.

Similarly, as Prochaska and DiClemente (1983) have shown, people come into therapy at different stages of readiness to tackle their problems. For example, before instituting an action mode within the comic vision, such as assertiveness training, Mrs. B. has to first become aware of the way in which she is making a martyr of herself and what in her background predisposes her to do so. This process falls within the ironic mode, where an effort is made to discern a deeper reality, hidden by superficial appearance. She then could be helped to see how she is overly deferential in interpersonal situations, including in her interactions with the therapist. At that point, she may become more ready to look out for her own needs, not just those of others, and could be taught through role playing, for example, how to better manage her interpersonal environment.

In these examples, we see a sequencing in use of the visions. At other times, the therapist may rapidly tack back and forth among the four visions in response to the shifting moods and needs of the client. The examples illustrate how taking into account contrasting and even contradictory theoretical perspectives can surpass what can be achieved using one or two perspectives only.

HISTORICAL AND EPISTEMOLOGICAL CONSIDERATIONS IN THE SEARCH FOR UNITY IN APPLIED PSYCHOLOGY

Pragmatic psychology, illustrated by the case of Mrs. B., is a new, bottom-up approach to unity in applied psychology. It emerges from a search for a third way out of psychology's present "culture wars" between modern–positivist and postmodern–constructivist visions of psychology. These culture wars undermine unity in applied psychology and draw resources away from practical problem solving that is directed toward today's pressing psychological and social issues. Next we describe the culture wars and pragmatic psychology as one way of resolving them.

The Modern, Positivist Vision of Unity

Positivism assumes that a fundamental set of underlying, unifying laws of human behavior and experience can be discovered from the natural-science-derived experimental method. Following a model of applied psychology that Peterson (1997) calls "applied science," positivists believe that once the underlying laws are uncovered, they can be used to deductively derive technologies for helping applied psychology's "clients"—from individuals to communities—to address the problems for which they seek help. Thus, for the positivist, creating unity in applied psychology can be traced back to discovering the fundamental laws of psychological functioning through psychological science.

One dramatic example of the positivist search for the basic, underlying laws of psychology is the work of the learning theorist Clark Hull. In the spirit of Isaac Newton and his superunifying formulas (e.g., $f = ma$), in 1943 Hull presented a general mathematical model of *all* animal and human action, which he notated as $sEr = sHr \times D \times V \times K$. This translates into a statement that the likelihood of a particular behavior (sEr) in regard to a particular reward or goal depends on how habitual the behavior is (sHr), how motivated or driven the organism is to seek the reward (D), how intense the stimulus signaling the reward is (V), and how much of the reward may come as a consequence of the behavior (K). From the formula Hull was able to derive 17 postulates that could be combined into 133 specific theorems and numerous corollaries. This looked impressive in terms of the natural science model. The only problem was that as the theory's testable propositions were researched in the laboratory, they repeatedly failed to yield confirming data.

Although stop-gap corrections kept the theory afloat for a time, Hull's students and collaborators finally acknowledged failure after his death (Baars, 1986).

Judged by today's sensibilities, Hull's efforts to explain the vast diversity of human behavior on the basis of the behavior of animals in the laboratory seems simplistic and somewhat quaint. Of course, it should be noted that using animal behavior as the basis for generalization still lives today within the evolutionary psychology movement (Pinker, 1999). However, evolutionary psychology is viewed as one of many possible approaches to psychology, not the *only* approach accepted by all.

Thirty-five years after Hull, another psychologist took the dream of a fully unified psychology for another breathtaking spin. In the spirit of Hull, but bringing to the table a much more complex and sophisticated basic paradigm informed by both biology and all of the social sciences, James G. Miller (1978) published his classic *Living Systems*. In it, he tried to show that a general theory of living systems could be constructed. Miller's book is an 1,102-page *tour de force* that demonstrates the conceptual and functional parallels among seven levels of systems: the cell, the organ, the individual organism, the group, the organization, the society, and the supranational system. Miller laid out 19 critical subsystems within each of the seven systems, which created 133 categories of knowledge, together with an additional category that involved how interactions of matter, energy, and information among systems at one level could be conceptualized as creating the next higher level. Cross-cutting these 134 categories were 186 hypotheses for testing.

Part of Miller's *magnum opus* was to fit vast amounts of the published research literature from biology and each of the social sciences into his 134 knowledge categories and 186 hypotheses. The scope of this feat is indicated by the fact that Miller's index of authors had 2,400 entries. However, although Miller's book was something of a sensation at the time of its publication, it is rarely mentioned today. When it is cited, it is more for its detailed presentation of system concepts, not because of new data in support of its empirical hypotheses. Also, no individual or group has attempted to update the book by incorporating into its framework empirical work conducted since 1978. One explanation for the failure of Miller's vision to have a long life in the history of psychology's unification efforts is that it took place in the middle of a postmodern period of increasing diversity, pluralism, and perspectivism in psychology, as discussed more later in the chapter. In this light, Miller's grand, systems theory integration of all social science knowledge is today viewed—like evolutionary psychology mentioned earlier—as one of a number of different possible paradigmatic perspectives. In other words, it is seen as one possible, historically interesting attempt at integration, but not the one "true" attempt at integration accepted by all.

The Postmodern, Constructivist Vision of Fragmentation and Antifoundationalism

One important reason for the decline of interest in grand unifying efforts such as Hull's and J. G. Miller's has been the rise in psychology and the other social sciences of an alternative to positivism: the postmodern, constructivist epistemological paradigm, starting in the early 1960s and inspired by continental philosophy. The established modern, positivist view is guided by the assumption that a single, objectively knowable psychosocial world—organized by quantitative, "context-free," and "value-free" laws— is being progressively discovered by dispassionate social scientists through rigorous application of the experimental or quasi-experimental method to the study of groups of subjects. By contrast, postmodern epistemology embod- ies an opposite view in every way: Psychosocial knowledge must be con- structed through naturalistic observation, not discovered experimentally, and it is intrinsically subjective, perspectival, context-bound, valuative, fragmented, nonfoundational, and reflective of multiple realities (Denzin & Lincoln, 2000; Fishman, 1999; Gergen, 2000). For example, consider the postmodern approach to social science research as described by Denzin and Lincoln, editors of the highly regarded book on this topic, the *Handbook of Qualitative Research:*

> [Postmodern social scientists primarily employ qualitative methods that range] from grounded theory to the case study, to methods of historical, biographical, ethnographic, action, and clinical research.... [Their theories vary] from symbolic interactions to constructivism, naturalistic inquiry, ... phenomenology, ethnomethodology, critical theory, neo- Marxist theory, semiotics, structuralism, feminism, and various racial/ ethnic paradigms.... The old functional, positivist, behavioral, totaliz- ing approaches to the human disciplines ... [have been] giving way to a more pluralistic, interpretive, open-ended perspective, [including] "thick descriptions" of particular events, rituals, and customs.... [with] boundaries between the social sciences and the humanities [becoming] ... blurred. (2000, p. 15)

Other Forces Working Against Positivist-Inspired Unity

Starting in the 1930s and continuing into the 1970s, positivism was also being challenged from within its ranks by Anglo American "postpositivist" philosophical ideas:

Popper, Kuhn, Quine, Feyerabend, and Wittgenstein all sound a similar theme, emphasizing the limitations if not the impossibility of objective, scientific knowledge because of our embeddedness in the logical, cultural, cognitive, and linguistic preconditions of that knowledge—preconditions that change according to historical and cultural context. For Popper, these preconditions include the deductive theoretical principles that we simply have to assume without being able to prove them; for Kuhn, these preconditions are scientific paradigms; for Quine and Feyerabend, they are webs of belief; and for Wittgenstein, they are language games. (Fishman, 1999, pp. 87–88)

The move toward postmodernism and postpositivism in psychology was part of a larger "centrifugal" trend in society toward diversity, starting in the early 1960s, after a period of relative cultural unity from the late 19th century. For example, since the 1960s there has been (a) an explosion in the number and types of members within, and in the types of specialties recognized by the American Psychological Association; (b) the development of dramatically new psychological perspectives, such as humanistic psychology, the cognitive revolution, and a focus on the impact of human diversity; and (c) the development of new epistemological and methodological perspectives in psychology, such as hermeneutics, social constructionism, qualitative research, and feminist research approaches, and the separation of "human science" from "natural science" (Altman, 1987).

Pragmatic Psychology as a "Third Way" in Applied Psychology

As a group, the broad, dispersive forces just outlined have worked in opposition to unity in psychology. More specifically, postmodernism has contributed to fragmentation in psychology in two ways. First, the dialectical opposition of modernism and postmodernism has created its own "culture wars" in psychology, especially because postmodernism focuses much of its energies on ideological and intellectual opposition to positivism (Messer, Sass, & Woolfolk, 1988). Second, as mentioned earlier, postmodernism is intrinsically committed to disciplinary knowledge that is in many ways foundationless, fragmentary, relativist, and dependent on the perspective of the knower.

Postmodernism's fragmenting, dialectical struggle with positivist-inspired models certainly rules out straightforward unity in psychology in Hull's and J. G. Miller's sense. Attacks on the possibility of discovering an agreed-on set of underlying laws of human behavior are also attacks on the viability of the applied science model for unifying applied psychology. If basic researchers cannot come to an agreement on the underlying laws of human behavior, there is no resulting base on which to deductively derive applied psychology technologies for the effective amelioration of human problems. However, we believe that there is a "third" way. This is "pragmatic psychology" and its associated pragmatic case study method. This approach draws on, in a complementary and integrative manner, the insights of both postmodernism and positivism to create a unifying framework for applied psychological research generally and psychotherapy research specifically. As mentioned at the start of the chapter, the PCS method does this by a bottom-up inductive approach, in direct contrast to the top-down deductive model of applied science.

Pragmatic psychology is an applied psychology model that is grounded in philosophical pragmatism—first developed in the late 19th century by such thinkers as William James, Charles Peirce, and John Dewey (Menand, 2002) and later elaborated on by such postmodern thinkers as Richard Bernstein (1983), Richard Rorty (1991), and Stephen Toulmin (1990). James's and Dewey's philosophical pragmatism is founded on a social constructionist theory of knowledge, which is why it has been embraced by a number of postmodern thinkers. One of pragmatism's organizing themes is the concept of contextualism:

> The world is seen as an unlimited complex of change and novelty, order and disorder. Out of this total flux we select certain contexts; these contexts serve as organizing gestalts or patterns that give meaning and scope to the vast array of details that, without the organizing pattern, would be meaningless or invisible. (Lilienfeld, 1978, p. 9)

In other words, to understand and cope with the world, we take on different conceptual perspectives, as we might put on different pairs of glasses, with each providing a different perspective on the world. The pragmatic "truth" of a particular perspective does not lie in its correspondence with "objective reality," because that reality is continuously in flux. Rather, pragmatic truth lies in the usefulness of the perspective in helping us to solve particular problems and achieve particular goals in today's world.

How are these problems and goals to be selected, defined, articulated, and addressed? The social constructionist epistemology of postmodernism proposes that human problems and goals are not "given" by the natural world, and thus they cannot be discovered through rational thought, as moral objectivists claim, or through natural science as evolutionary psychologists, among others, claim. Instead, these problems and goals represent the multiple purposes, intentions, desires, interests, and values of individuals and groups. In most industrialized Western countries there is a political and moral consensus that these problems and goals should be articulated and chosen through dialogue and democratically negotiated agreement among the local individuals, groups, and communities who are stakeholders in the particular problems and goals involved.

As a constructionist, problem-solving-centered epistemology, pragmatism rejects the notion of foundational truths, but it does present an alternative to "anything goes" relativism—that is, to the undermining of any standards for deciding what is true or false, good or bad. This alternative, "pragmatic relativism" (Fishman, 1999), while denying transhistorical and cross-cultural "foundational" standards, points to the already established and agreed-on procedures and norms Western society now has for determining truth and morality in particular contexts (Putnam, 1981). Examples are the procedures and standards used to elect government officials democratically, to settle civil and criminal disputes in the court system, to conduct academic scholarship in universities, to carry out investigative journalism, and to describe social behavior "objectively" in quantitative surveys such as the U.S. Census, using the statistical methods derived from natural science.

In summary, philosophical pragmatism holds that applied knowledge is not "given" by nature but rather is constructed in specific human contexts to solve particular problems, ideally as democratically agreed on by relevant stakeholders. Building on this way of thinking, pragmatic psychology proposes that in deciding on what should be the basic unit of knowledge in applied psychology, we should start from the point at which knowledge is ultimately applied. That end point is the single, holistically situated case, because the ultimate purpose of applied psychological knowledge is to improve the condition of actual clients within the complexities of their reality, whether the "client" be an individual, a family, a group, an organization, or a community (Fishman & Neigher, 2003).

It has been argued that knowledge of a single case lacks "external validity"—that is, the capacity to generalize in a deductive manner, which one can do within the positivist paradigm via the group experimental study. Nevertheless, the single case study does contain the potential to *inductively* generalize across settings (Fishman, 1999). This can come about by organizing case studies of clients with similar target goals and similar intervention approaches into computerized databases. For example, consider the application of cognitive–behavioral therapy to a phobia in a middle-class, professional Latina woman who has associated depressive symptoms, marital difficulties, and alcohol problems. Or consider family therapy with a poor, White teenager who is also a single mother of a child with attention deficit disorder. A write-up of either case is limited in terms of the number of case situations in the future to which it will apply. This limitation is a result of large contextual differences that can occur between any one case and any other case that is randomly drawn out of a heterogeneous case pool. However, as cases in the database grow, they begin to sample a wide variety of contextually different situations in which the target problem can occur and a wide variety of intervention approaches for that problem. Therefore, as the number of cases in the database rises substantially, the probability increases that there exist specific cases in the database that are particularly relevant to a new target case in terms of both the nature of the target problem and the intervention approach used.

Thus, pragmatic psychology, through the PCS method, calls for the creation of databases of systematic case studies. To create such databases at the highest level of scholarship, Fishman (2000, 2001) has called for the creation of peer-reviewed journal–databases. These would be online journals to accommodate, first, large numbers of thickly described cases and, second, easy accessibility to search the considerable amount of qualitative and quantitative material in the cases. Also, such a journal would be structured like a wheel, to accommodate the developing "bootstraps" nature of case study knowledge:

> The hub of the wheel would consist of articles of two types: (a) those that address epistemological, theoretical, methodological, logistical, economic, political, and ethical issues in the development of insightful and useful, systematic case studies in the problem area; and (b) substantive cross-case analyses of groups of individual cases already published in the database. The spokes of the wheel would each consist of particular databases of types of cases within the content area, embodying the issues and applied usefulness associated with practice in the content area. (2001, p. 299)

At the Graduate School of Applied and Professional Psychology at Rutgers, we are about to launch a pilot-test of this concept with an online journal, *Pragmatic Case Studies in Psychotherapy*. (For more information about this journal, contact the first author.)

To facilitate analysis across cases in our new journal, it is important to have a common and standardized, but still quite generic, framework for structuring case study write-ups. As an initial base for this, we have chosen Peterson's (1997) disciplined inquiry model, which is based in part on empirical studies of how the most effective professionals in diverse fields actually practice (Schön, 1983) and which Peterson contrasts with the applied science model used by followers of Hull and J. G. Miller as mentioned previously.

Unlike the positivist approach to applied psychology, which begins with research on basic principles and then uses these principles to create technologies for application to clients, the disciplined inquiry model begins with the client, his or her problems, and goals for change. The first step is assessment, which is orchestrated by (a) the practitioner's "guiding conception" of the process under study, including assumptions about theory, epistemology, intervention program goals, and ethics; and (b) the practitioner's knowledge of relevant empirical research and remembered examples of similar cases. The assessment is then used by the practitioner to create a specific formulation of the client's situation and an action plan for change. This is followed by actual intervention, the effects of which are monitored in an ongoing manner. The results of the monitoring can lead to the possibility of recycling to the earlier steps; for example, lack of progress toward goals might lead to a reassessment and/or a reformulation of the client's problems. When the process is completed, a concluding evaluation can be conducted to assess the overall outcome of the intervention.

Linking the Pragmatic Case Study Method to Basic Research

Although the main focus of this chapter is unification in applied psychology through pragmatic psychology, it should be noted that there are links between pragmatic psychology ideas and unification efforts in basic research.

Theories as Wittgensteinian "Tools"

The disciplined inquiry model incorporates both positivist and postmodern basic research—as they apply to a particular client—in its "guiding conception" component. More generally, adding to overarching unification, pragmatic psychology views the theories, methods, and empirical results of both positivist and postmodern psychology as tools that can be usefully applied to certain types of cases and case situations, including multiple theories used in a complementary manner. (This is like Wittgenstein's analogy of language as similar to a bag of carpenter's tools, with each having its relevance and value in certain types of situations.) For example, the pragmatist views positivists as having contributed psychometrically sophisticated and inventive methodologies that set high standards for rigorous, critical, and ingenious thinking about the complexities of measuring psychological phenomena. They have developed a rich supply of psychological theories and ideas that explore the vast array of possible perspectives that can be taken on human behavior and action.

Parallels Between the Case and Sternberg's "Phenomena" as Unifying Vehicles in Psychology

As discussed and illustrated earlier in the case of Mrs. B., the logic of pragmatic psychology for unification in applied psychology parallels that of Sternberg and his colleagues (2001), who argued that unification in basic research can be enhanced by creating a psychology that is phenomenon-oriented rather than theory-based, that is multi- rather than monoparadigmatic, and multi- rather than monomethod.

Ragin's "Fuzzy-Set Social Science"

The sociologist Charles Ragin (2000) has demonstrated that a useful approach in basic social science research is to use combined qualitative and quantitative data from the multivariate case as the fundamental unit of data collection and analysis. This is in contrast to the traditional model, which uses individual variables abstracted from a large number of individual cases. Ragin shows that an important consequence of his model is that seemingly similar cases at the variable level can actually divide into a variety of subtypes at the case level, with each subtype possessing a different causal model for how a system's inputs and activities are related to its outcomes.

Ragin's work has engendered a great deal of international interest and involvement, which has been organized around a COMPASSS Research Group (COMParative methods for the Advancement of Systematic cross-case analysis and Small-n Studies). The resonance of this effort with the theme of the case as a vehicle for unity discussed earlier can be seen in the description on their Web site:

> COMPASSS is a research group bringing together scholars and prac-titioners who share a common interest in theoretical, methodological and practical advancements in a systematic comparative case approach to research which stresses the use of a configurational logic, the existence of multiple causality and the importance of a careful construction of research populations.
>
> This site is open to all, regardless of disciplinary affiliation. Indeed, one key goal of this site is to bring together researchers and practitioners from a broad range of disciplines (political science, sociology, anthropol-ogy, economics, law, history, social work, demography, marriage and family therapy, criminology, psychology, education science, etc.). (COMPASS Research Group, 2004)

EFFORTS TOWARD UNITY IN PSYCHOTHERAPY RESEARCH AND PRACTICE

We now turn to illustrating this viewpoint within the arena of psycho-therapy research and practice. Psychotherapy is well-known for its fragmen-tation, with the existence of hundreds of contrasting psychotherapy ap-proaches or "schools" (Karasu, 1986). Whereas in the single-school approach to treatment a therapist adheres to a particular theory and uses the interven-tions that are prescribed by it, psychotherapy integration refers to the effort to look beyond one school and to incorporate theories and strategies from other models. To explore current developments in psychotherapy integra-tion, especially as they affect the use of the case study in the integrative process, we next take a brief critical look at three major efforts to unify psychotherapy: the search for common factors across therapies, technical eclecticism, and theoretical integration.

Common Factors

This way of seeking integration looks for commonality across the different therapies, most typically in their practices but also in their theories. It is based on the premise that there is much more held in common by the different brands of therapy than that which is dissimilar. This perspective has been strongly bolstered by the repeated result of "no difference" in comparative therapy outcome studies (e.g., Luborsky et al., 2002). In addition, the finding that only a relatively small percentage of the outcome variance in psychotherapy is a result of specific techniques compared to client, therapist, and interpersonal factors (e.g., Lambert, 1992) has also accelerated the search for common factors.

Perhaps the best known attempt to present the common factors in any kind of psychotherapy is that of Jerome Frank (e.g., Frank, Frank, & Cousins, 1993). According to Frank, the patient enters therapy in a state of demoralization—that is, disheartened and dispirited. All therapeutic systems, he postulated, combat demoralization through the provision of four effective features (Frank & Frank, 1991, pp. 42–44): (a) an emotionally charged, confiding relationship with a helping person; (b) a healing setting; (c) a rationale or conceptual scheme; and (d) a ritual or procedure that requires the active participation of both patient and therapist.

There is considerable appeal in the prospect of a therapy model that teases out the factors that contribute to successful outcomes in many or all therapies. This approach has the virtue of pragmatism and unifying parsimony, as well as being consistent with the general research literature on psychotherapy outcome. By emphasizing what the psychotherapies share rather than what separates them, common change principles provide a meeting ground for proponents of different schools, thereby promoting a more open, unified, and less doctrinaire stance. However there is no guarantee that we have correctly discerned what are the most efficacious common factors and, therefore, cannot confidently advocate which ones should be emphasized. For example, in an analysis of 50 studies (Grencavage & Norcross, 1990), only 50% of the authors reviewed cited the most popular candidate—the development of the therapeutic alliance. Other factors were agreed on only by 24% to 38% of the sample.

Another problem is the lack of specificity of the common factors. The level of generality in which they are stated may allow initial agreement about their commonality, but on closer inspection they look quite different across therapies. For example, although the therapeutic alliance is an important common factor, both the formation and the nature of the alliance will differ for different individuals, in different therapies, that have varied purposes and goals. We suggest that applying the inductive, PCS method to study common factors in depth and in context would effectively address this present weakness in the common factors literature.

Technical Eclecticism

Eclectic therapists are prepared to draw on techniques from any source if they seem called for in a particular case. The emphasis in technical eclecticism is on what works, preferably as determined by empirical research. Theory is accorded less importance. In Lazarus's (1992) brand of technical eclecticism, for example, a client's problems are assessed across seven descriptive categories: behavior, affect, sensation, imagery, cognition, interpersonal relationships, and drugs/biology. Interventions are chosen to target each problem in each modality. It is Lazarus's contention that one can incorporate diverse techniques without bringing along pieces of the theoretical framework in which they are embedded (Lazarus, in Lazarus & Messer, 1991).

Technical eclecticism has the virtue of pragmatism, calling on what works regardless of the dictates of a particular theory. It is empirically oriented, paying attention to what has been learned from research or clinical practice even more so than from theory. It takes clients' (and, to a lesser extent, therapists') individuality seriously by attempting to tailor the therapy to their particular needs. Furthermore, it encourages therapists to think systematically about what kinds of treatments or individual techniques may apply to the clients in their care.

One of the problems with this form of eclecticism is the assumption that the usefulness of a given technique can be evaluated independently of the theory that gave rise to it (Lazarus, in Lazarus & Messer, 1991). It often proceeds as if a therapeutic technique is a disembodied procedure that can be readily transported from one context to another, much like a medical procedure, without consideration of its new psychotherapeutic context (Messer, in Lazarus & Messer, 1991). Yet, in line with the discussion earlier of contextualism, a therapeutic procedure such as an interpretation or an empathic response does not stand on its own independent of the framework of meaning created by the entire therapeutic system, as embodied in the relationship between a particular therapist and client. Although transported interventions can be effective, it is important that the new context is conveyed to and understood by the client. That is, the way in which a technique is assimilated into the home therapy is important because there is a pervasive effect of the theory used (Messer, 2001). In summary, it is a feature of the PCS approach that we are proposing that it is intrinsically context-based and thus is ideally suited to take into account a therapist's theoretical framing of a case and what he or she is bringing to the table.

Theoretical Integration

In this form of integration, different theories are combined in the attempt to produce a superior, overarching conceptual framework for psychotherapy. Perhaps the best known example of theoretical integration is Wachtel's (1997) rapprochement of interpersonal psychodynamic therapy and behavior therapy, based on cyclical psychodynamic theory. On the positive side, such superordinate integrative theories can lead to new and valuable forms of therapy that capitalize on the strengths of each of its elements.

Theoretical integration also comes up against obstacles. For example, any theoretical integration picks and chooses which elements of each school it includes. Inevitably, elements that may be just as important as those embraced are excluded. Whether one judges an integrative therapy to be superior to the individual therapies from which it stems will depend on one's view of the importance of the elements included and excluded. In light of what we have discussed, we suggest that the search for a *single* theory integrating all of psychotherapy is as problematic as Hull's and J. G. Miller's grand theories of integration. On the other hand, we welcome the development of new psychotherapy theories that integrate elements from present theories. The ultimate practical value of such integrative theories can then be contextually tested in the crucible of numbers of detailed, systematic psychotherapy case studies.

CONCLUSION

In going from unification via the individual therapy case of Mrs. B. to Miller's grand unification of the social sciences and biology, one might wonder if we are talking about the same discipline. Yes, we believe that these two examples dramatize the difference between a top-down versus a bottom-up approach to unity in applied psychology. We have argued that the advent of postmodern, postpositivist, and pluralistic perspectives in psychology has undermined the top-down, positivist approach to unification represented by Miller's model. However, we have also argued that a third way to such unity is possible via a bottom-up strategy that draws on both positivist and postmodern elements and themes. This is the pragmatic case study method, which proposes the creation of peer-reviewed journal–databases of systematic case studies in applied psychology areas such as psychotherapy, allowing for unifying themes within areas to emerge inductively through cross-case analysis. An important strength of the PCS method from a unifying point of view is its resonance with parallel efforts in the basic research arena by authors such as Sternberg et al. (2001) and Ragin (2000), who start with case-based phenomena and then derive inductively multiple, complementary theories for explaining such phenomena in a unified way. In short, we have argued in this chapter that, to paraphrase the old Chinese saying, the long journey to unity in applied psychology starts with a single, individual case.

REFERENCES

Altman, I. (1987). Centripetal and centrifugal trends in psychology. *American Psychologist, 42,* 1058–1069.

American Psychiatric Association. (1994). *Diagnostic and statistical manual of mental disorders* (4th ed.). Washington, DC: Author.

Andrews, J. D. W. (1989). Integrating visions of reality: Interpersonal diagnosis and the existential vision. *American Psychologist, 44,* 803–817.

Baars, B. J. (1986). *The cognitive revolution in psychology.* New York: Guilford Press.

Bernstein, R. J. (1983). *Beyond objectivism and realism.* Philadelphia: University of Pennsylvania Press.

COMPASSs Research Group (COMParative Methods for the Advancement of Systematic Cross-Case Analysis and Small-n Studies). Retrieved March 12, 2004, from www.compasss.org

Denzin, N. K., & Lincoln, Y. S. (Eds.). (2000). *Handbook of qualitative research* (2nd ed.). Thousand Oaks, CA: Sage.

Fishman, D. B. (1999). *The case for pragmatic psychology.* New York: New York University Press.

Fishman, D. B. (2000). Transcending the efficacy versus effectiveness research debate: Proposal for a new, electronic "Journal of Pragmatic Case Studies." *Prevention and Treatment, 3,* Article 8. Retrieved May 3, 2000, from http://journals.apa.org/prevention

Fishman, D. B. (2001). From single case to database: A new method for enhancing psychotherapy, forensic, and other psychological practice. *Applied and Preventive Psychology, 10,* 275–304.

Fishman, D. B., & Neigher, W. D. (2003). Publishing systematic, pragmatic case studies in program evaluation: Rationale and introduction to the special issue. *Evaluation and Program Planning, 26,* 421–428.

Frank, J. D., & Frank, J. B. (1991). *Persuasion and healing* (3rd ed.). Baltimore: Johns Hopkins University Press.

Frank, J. D., Frank, J. B., & Cousins, N. (1993). *Persuasion and healing: A comparative study of psychotherapy* (3rd ed.). Baltimore: Johns Hopkins University Press.

Frye, N. (1957). *Anatomy of criticism*. New York: Athenaeum.

Gergen, K. J. (2000). *The saturated self*. New York: Basic Books.

Grencavage, L. M., & Norcross, J. C. (1990). Where are the commonalities among the therapeutic common factors? *Professional Psychology, 21*, 372–378.

Hull, C. L. (1943). *Principles of behavior*. New York: Appleton-Century-Crofts.

Karasu, T. B. (1986). The specificity versus nonspecificity dilemma: Toward identifying therapeutic change agents. *American Journal of Psychiatry, 143*, 687–695.

Lambert, M. J. (1992). Psychotherapy outcome research: Implications for integrative and eclectic therapists. In J. C. Norcross & M. R. Goldfried (Eds.), *Handbook of psychotherapy integration* (pp. 94–129). New York: Basic Books.

Lazarus, A. A. (1992). Multimodal therapy: Technical eclecticism with minimal integration. In J. C. Norcross & M. R. Goldfried (Eds.), *Handbook of psychotherapy integration* (pp. 231–263). New York: Basic Books.

Lazarus, A. A., & Messer, S. B. (1991). Does chaos prevail? An exchange on technical eclecticism and assimilative integration. *Journal of Psychotherapy Integration, 1*, 143–158.

Lilienfeld, R. (1978). *The rise of systems theory: An ideological analysis*. New York: John Wiley.

Luborsky, L., Rosenthal, R., Diguer, L., Andrusyna, T. P., Berman, J. S., Levitt, J. T., et al. (2002). The Dodo bird verdict is alive and well—mostly. *Clinical psychology: Science and Practice, 9*, 2–12.

Menand, L. (2002). *The metaphysical club: A story of ideas in America*. New York: Farrar Straus & Giroux.

Messer, S. B. (2000). Applying the visions of reality to a case of brief therapy. *Journal of Psychotherapy Integration, 10*, 55–70.

Messer, S. B. (2001). Introduction to the special issue on assimilative integration. *Journal of Psychotherapy Integration, 11*, 1–4.

Messer, S. B., Sass, L. A., & Woolfolk, R. L. (Eds.). (1988). *Hermeneutics and psychological theory*. New Brunswick, NJ: Rutgers University Press.

Messer, S. B., & Winokur, M. (1984). Ways of knowing and visions of reality in psychoanalytic therapy and behavior therapy. In S. B. Messer & H. Arkowitz (Eds.), *Psychoanalytic therapy and behavior therapy: Is integration possible?* (pp. 63–100). New York: Plenum Press.

Messer, S. B., & Woolfolk, R. L. (1998). Philosophical issues in psychotherapy. *Clinical Psychology: Science and Practice, 5*, 251–263.

Miller, J. G. (1978). *Living systems*. New York: McGraw-Hill.

Peterson, D. R. (1997). *Educating professional psychologists: History and guiding conception*. Washington, DC: American Psychological Association.

Pinker, S. (1999). *How the mind works*. New York: W.W. Norton.

Prochaska, J. O., & DiClemente, C. C. (1983). Stages and processes of self-change of smoking: Toward an integrative model of change. *Journal of Consulting and Clinical Psychology, 51*, 390–395.

Putnam, H. (1981). *Reason, truth, and history*. New York: Cambridge University Press.

Ragin, C. C. (2000). *Fuzzy-set social science*. Chicago: University of Chicago Press.

Rorty, R. (1991). *Objectivity, relativism, and truth*. New York: Cambridge University Press.

Schafer, R. (1976). *A new language for psychoanalysis*. New Haven, CT: Yale University Press.

Schön, D. A. (1983). *The reflective practitioner: How professionals think in action*. New York: Basic Books.

Sternberg, R. J., Grigorenko, E. L., & Kalmar, D. A. (2001). The role of theory in unified psychology. *Journal of Theoretical and Philosophical Psychology, 21*, 99–117.

Task Force on Promotion and Dissemination of Psychological Procedures. (1995). Training and dissemination of empirically-validated psychological treatment: Report and recommendations. *Clinical Psychologist, 48*, 2–23.

Toulmin, S. (1990). *Cosmopolis: The hidden agenda of modernity*. Chicago: University of Chicago Press.

Wachtel, P. L. (1997). *Psychoanalysis, behavior therapy, and the relational world*. Washington, DC: American Psychological Association.

Wile, D. B. (1984). Kohut, Kernberg, and accusatory interpretations. *Psychotherapy, 22*, 793–802.

4

THE AMERICAN PSYCHOLOGICAL ASSOCIATION AND THE SEARCH FOR UNITY IN PSYCHOLOGY

RAYMOND D. FOWLER AND MERRY BULLOCK

For more than a century, the American Psychological Association (APA) has been the primary scientific and professional organization representing U.S. psychologists. There are a number of psychological organizations in the United States, but the APA is the largest and the only one that represents the entire range of psychologists. The APA's size and influence permit it to undertake the responsibilities of promoting psychology as a discipline, as a profession, and as a science, and of representing psychology to the broader national and international publics. From its founding, the APA has served a unifying function for psychology; but in a discipline both so broad and so diverse there are strong tendencies toward fragmentation.

Psychology did not begin as a unified discipline. Although scholars were engaged in research and writing on psychological topics, there was no generally recognized discipline of psychology, no identification of the people who were working in psychology, and no established lines of communication. The early researchers came from several disciplines, including education, philosophy, religion, physiology, medicine, and biology. These scholars brought the concepts of several disciplines to bear on the understanding of behavior and thinking. The establishment of the APA provided them with an opportunity to interact with each other and brought identity and recognition to the discipline. To appreciate the APA's role in the promotion of unity within psychology requires an understanding of the evolution of psychology as a discipline, the forces that have worked to bring it together and to fragment it, and the various forms that fragmentation has taken.

In this chapter, we examine the unity of psychology as embodied in the evolution of the APA as an association of psychologists. To capture this evolution, we will examine the forces that have threatened the status of psychology as a coherent discipline and profession—conceptual challenges to unity, science–practice divergence, and organizational challenges. Throughout, we will describe the role that the APA has played in each of these arenas, focusing on ways that its activities have promoted unity. We will conclude by examining how the APA's current role as the umbrella organization for psychology serves to encourage unity now, and will continue to do so into the future.

CONCEPTUAL CHALLENGES TO A UNIFIED DISCIPLINE OF PSYCHOLOGY

Concerns about the fragmentation of psychology and efforts to promote the unity of psychology are themes that have appeared and reappeared for at least 100 years. The remarkable breadth of psychology's subject matter and the range of its methods have led some to believe that it is not a single discipline but a collection of areas of study. Whether one looks for unity in a discipline's content (its subject matter, models, and theories) or in a discipline's world view and approach (its language, laws, and methods), the critical question for many in psychology is, Can psychology be a unified discipline?

How should we address this question? Sigmund Koch, one of the first scholars to examine the question systematically, was designated by the APA and the National Science Foundation to assess the status of psychology as a science. The results of his inquiry, published in 1959 as *Psychology: A Study of a Science*, and reflected in his *Psychology Today* article a decade later (1969), were that "psychology *cannot* be a coherent science or indeed a coherent field of scholarship" (p. 65, emphasis in original) because the subject matter is simply too broad. "Anything so awesome as the total domain comprised by the functioning of all organisms," he said, "can hardly be thought to be the subject matter of a coherent discipline" (p. 65).

Others have seen fragmentation as a perfectly natural outgrowth of the maturing of a science. For example, Gordon Bower observed,

A science grows over time by covering more ground, taking up new but related problems to attack, distinguishing between cases and differentiating among types of things or topics that were formerly lumped together, obtaining new findings, and then elaborating new concepts and theories around them. (1993, p. 905)

He went on to add that this specialization was not necessarily negative, asserting that "most people don't think specialization is so bad, especially when they need a doctor who specializes in what ails them" (p. 906).

Similarly, Arthur Staats in his book, *Psychology's Crisis of Disunity*, acknowledged fragmentation but believed unity was attainable. He observed that "what psychology has achieved in its 100 or so years of self conscious striving, does provide the raw materials for making the leap to the status of a unified science" (1983, p. vi).

Koch's cautions still echo one of the major challenges to psychology: the complexity and multifaceted nature of behavior stretches the explanatory power of any single paradigm or single model. But psychology, like other sciences, has made great strides in addressing complexity. New methodologies allow a more coherent understanding of complex phenomena, so that domains that once were thought to "belong" to other disciplines can be studied and addressed within psychology. Examples include the behavior of communities; behavioral genetics and social contexts; and multilevel, multivariable behavioral systems that can be modelled through new mathematical and statistical tools.

At the same time, the coherence of psychology is challenged by the rapid development of allied areas that cross disciplinary boundaries and are represented in independent academic departments. These include neuroscience, cognitive science, behavioral genetics, and family studies, to name a few. For each of these areas, the discipline of psychology, with its unique history, methods, and assumptions, is but one thread among many.

SCIENCE–PRACTICE DIVERGENCE AS A CHALLENGE TO UNITY

Just as fragmentation or specialization in subject matter, methods, and theories challenges the unity of psychology as a discipline, so too do the two sides of psychology—its science and its practice—pose a challenge. In the early years of psychology, the focus was on building a science base for the discipline, with little attention to the application of the discipline or the training of practitioners. But it is clear from the addresses of the earliest presidents of the APA and their contemporaries that they foresaw the development of a profession of psychology that could use the knowledge base of psychological science to benefit humanity and that they recognized that many of the questions informing the most basic research derived from a pragmatic, applied need. G. Stanley Hall, the APA's founder, taught child development to physicians to help them understand and more appropriately treat their child patients. William James taught teachers to apply psychological principles to classroom teaching and was among the earliest proponents of psychotherapy as an effective way to reduce human misery. George Ladd (1894), the APA's second president, foresaw the application of psychology to education, neurology, criminal justice, and family relations. James McKeen Cattell, the APA's fourth president, published the first psychological testing program in 1890. A firm believer that psychological science could contribute to the public good, he said, "The measurement and statistics of psychology, which, at first sight, may seem remote from the common interest, may in the end become the most important factor in the progress of society" (quoted in Roback, 1952, p. 174). In 1937, 41 years after his presidency, Cattell was asked to comment on psychology as a profession in the first issue of the *Journal of Consulting Psychology*. He said,

> All of the professions need a science of psychology and a profession of psychology. The present function of a physician, a lawyer, a clergyman, a teacher or a man of business is to a considerable extent that of an amateur psychologist. In the inevitable specialization of modern society, there will become increasing need of those who can be paid for expert psychological advice. . . . In the end, there will be not only a science but also a profession of psychology. (1937, p. 3)

At the time Cattell spoke, most of the APA's 3,000 members were employed in academic settings. During the years following World War II, the profession of psychology began to expand. Thousands of veterans, supported by generous federal education grants, were attracted to industrial, organizational, school, and clinical psychology. Soon the majority of new graduates were in the applied fields. This pattern is characteristic of all of the scientific disciplines. The predominant opportunities for employment in psychology and in some other disciplines shifted from the university to business, government, consulting, and the delivery of services.

Some psychologists viewed the rapid development of professional psychology as a threat to the development of psychology as a science. But it may be argued that the development of professional psychology helped to strengthen and advance scientific psychology. The increased visibility of psychology as an applied discipline brought increased resources available to academic departments in the form of research grants and new positions. During both world wars, but especially during World War II, psychologists demonstrated that the knowledge base of psychology could be applied to the nation's benefit. This demonstration increased psychology's public acceptance and helped to justify the claim that additional research could result in still more benefits to the nation.

In the postwar years, psychology received a great deal of attention from the national media. Television, motion pictures, magazines, and newspapers featured psychologists and their work, and psychology became a household word throughout the country. This national enthusiasm for psychology attracted undergraduate and graduate students in unprecedented numbers. The growth in those social sciences that did not have applied or professional aspects was much more modest. Psychology departments grew in size and resources because of the growth of professional psychology, and the profession gained credibility because of its scientific foundation.

The growth of professional psychology took place during a period in which most of the new opportunities for employment occurred outside academic settings, especially in the health-care sector. Psychology did not change from being a science to being a profession. It would be more accurate to say that the changing face of American psychology involved the development of an additional face—a professional face—and not the demise of the already well-established academic-research face. Psychology did not *become* a profession; rather, psychology *added* a profession to the academic science foundation that already existed (Fowler, 1990).

As professional psychologists grew in numbers and influence, the conflict between scientists and practitioners increased. Psychologists primarily concerned with generating and dissemenating knowledge sometimes resented those psychologists whose primary concern was with the application of psychology. Scientists complained that practitioners did not publish much research and did not base their applications on the scientific literature. Practitioners argued that researchers did not inform themselves of the issues practitioners had to deal with and that the research produced by academicians was often irrelevant to real-life problems. As Bevan wrote, "We differ in motivation and goals and we won't find peace by glossing over those differences" (1982, p. 1310).

How does a profession build on science? Harrison (1984) pointed out that a profession can best build on science when there is a reciprocal relationship. In such a relationship, science supports a fundamental knowledge base to provide both skills and strategies for practice, and practice both fulfills the goals of service to society and provides a context for scientific inquiry into behavior.

The question that remains is how can we achieve the synergy that is necessary if psychology is to contribute what it has the potential to contribute? How can we develop that reciprocal relationship between the science and the profession and, more important, between scientists and professionals? Perhaps psychology could profit from a shift from preoccupation with our differences to an examination of how our diversity enriches psychology as a whole. Bevan (1982) commented that "the problems which ultimately will tax us most severely [are] the problems of balance and interrelatedness between our basic and applied concerns" (p. 1303). It seems to us that it is that *interrelatedness* that has been most seriously neglected to the detriment of the discipline (Fowler, 1990).

Kimble (1984) proposed that two distinct cultures exist within the discipline. His survey of the attitudes and views of psychologists revealed marked differences in professional and scientific values between scientists and practitioners. Achieving synergy of science–practice interaction is difficult because practitioners and scientists do not normally come together. With the exception of scientist–practitioners in academic settings, scientists and practitioners work in different settings, read different journals, and rank different issues as their highest priorities. Organizations that bring scientists and professionals together to deal with common issues are rare, but they can play an important role in creating interaction and synergy.

As an umbrella organization, the APA stands in a unique position to foster vehicles for interaction and synergy. There are many examples illustrating how the APA's convening power and its diverse membership serve to bring science and practice to the same table with common goals. One way in which this works is when scientists and practitioners share content interests. For example, the Committee on Testing and Assessment, the APA's oldest committee (founded in 1895), regularly addresses testing issues that are relevant to both practitioners and scientists and that require both practice and research expertise (e.g., testing on the Internet; observers in the test situation). In this case, the membership of the committee is mandated to ensure science and practice representation. Analogously, the interdirectorate Task Force on Promoting Resilience in Response to Terrorism, one of the APA's newest groups, fosters synergy as it brings together scientists and practitioners to explore what psychology can offer to policy makers who are grappling with new issues in prediction, communication, and treatment in large-scale, risky, crisis situations.

As an umbrella organization, the APA takes responsibility for developing standards for the discipline in such areas as ethics, testing, and methodologies and for developing policy on a broad range of issues from the applications of psychology to societal challenges to psychology's role in health decisions and psychology's concerns with legislative and regulatory oversight on research. Such standards require, before they are adopted, extensive study by members drawn from all aspects of psychology and approval by the Council of Representatives, which represents all of the APA's constituent groups. The APA also takes responsibility for providing to policy makers, the public, and psychologists information and judgments about controversial behavioral issues (such as the nature of intelligence, the status of recovered memories, and end-of-life care). In each of these areas, the APA's policy position may affect the scholarly, research, or professional work of its members. Thus, it is important to hear and represent the perspectives of broad and diverse constituencies. This affords an opportunity to bring scientists and practitioners together to address overarching issues.

It is not only the act of convening science and practice that facilitates interaction and unity. It is also the APA's consensus model of action and decision making within the organization. The consensus model means that groups, constituencies, and perspectives find a forum to be heard and to discuss issues until common ground is discovered or created. Practically, this means that scientists, practitioners, and others must inform, discuss with, and educate each other about their pieces of the pie and their perspectives on the discipline. The APA's complicated policy-approval system, which requires input from all relevant constituencies before granting approvals, has set in place both structures and a climate that encourage this process. Science and practice governance groups (boards and committees) are given an opportunity and obligation to read, comment, and reach consensus on each other's policy proposals before they become APA policy.

In addition to its governance structure and procedures, the APA promotes unity through its dissemination of scholarly activity. The APA publishes most of the major psychological journals and it archives and disseminates the world's psychological literature through its electronic databases. The two monthly publications every APA member receives—the *Monitor on Psychology* and the *American Psychologist*—present a broad picture of scientific and applied activities and thought as well as other issues. This encourages awareness by all members of the central issues across the entire discipline, not just one's own piece of it.

But the APA has also taken a more active role in trying to address real or perceived schisms between science and practice. In the 1950s the APA collaborated with the National Institutes of Mental Health to develop a scientist–practitioner training model for professional psychologists. Known as the Boulder model—after the city in which the conference was held—the scientist–practitioner approach to training was designed to help to integrate disparate sides of the discipline in one person. The Boulder model has remained the dominant approach to training in professional psychology in academic psychology departments for more than half a century. The scholar–practitioner model seen in many professional schools of psychology is a variation of the Boulder model that retains many of its integrative elements.

In more recent times, the APA fostered a program to increase interaction of academics and practitioners at the state level by encouraging academic departments and state psychological associations to coordinate their advocacy on policy issues and encouraging psychologists of all kinds to become active in APA governance. In the late 1990s, the APA's governing body, the Council of Representatives, mandated a Task Force on Science–Practice Integration that gathered material from a wide range of members, divisions, and governance constituencies, and made recommendations on how the APA could promote sharing and exchange across its many association activities.

Bold as these initiatives were, and impressive as the work of those who exemplify the scientist–practitioner model is, psychology has yet to achieve the integration that fueled the vision of a single, unified discipline, informed by science–practice synergies. This is not unique to psychology, but psychologists stand to play an important role in current efforts by funders and policy makers to foster "translation" and "translational research"—from neurons to neighborhoods. The APA can play an active role in that effort because of its unique position of commanding the attention of the entire range of psychologists in disseminating information, accrediting education and training, and fostering career development.

ORGANIZED PSYCHOLOGY AND UNITY

The founding of the APA in 1892 helped to identify psychology as a discipline and serves as a convenient marker for the beginning of a long trend in American psychology toward developing a large but unified discipline. This trend continued until the 1960s. Independent psychology departments emerged from philosophy departments, and the field consolidated. Behaviorism, experimentation, quantification, and logical positivism became the dominant frameworks for American psychology, and a coherent body of research began to develop. Before World War II, most psychologists were trained as experimental psychologists, and those primarily engaged in applying psychology were relatively few in number. World War II helped to further expand psychology and to bring increased visibility and respect to the applications of psychology.

The 1960s began a period of change in American society and the initiation of a trend in psychology that has characterized the subsequent four decades. This trend increased the tendencies toward fragmentation and instability in two of psychology's major institutions: the university psychology department and the APA. Before World War II, most psychology departments were small. Graduate students associated with each other and took many of the same courses, and faculty members were not differentiated into specialty areas. In the post-World War II years, psychology departments became larger, with many more faculty members and students. Faculty members and graduate students were grouped into the specialty areas, and departments changed from cohesive units to loosely affiliated bodies. This change resulted in much less interaction among students and faculty in different areas. Faculty members and students identified themselves less as psychologists and more as social psychologists or clinical psychologists, and so forth. This institutional fragmentation was also a factor in reducing the unitary nature of the major psychological organization, the APA.

The problem of defining psychology as a coherent discipline and the difficulties in integrating the scientific and applied wings of the discipline are reflected in the difficulty in maintaining a unitary national psychological organization. The founding of the APA, the world's first national psychological association, represented a unifying step because it brought together most of the people who identified themselves as psychologists.

But it should not be forgotten that although the establishment of a national organization helped to unify *psychology*, it also represented a step in the fragmentation of *science*. Before the late 1800s, scientific societies had been generic and broad-based. The prototype of such organizations, the American Association for the Advancement of Science (AAAS), founded in 1848, brought together scientists across all disciplines through its annual meetings and its publications. The establishment of the American Chemical Society in 1876 began a movement toward the splitting of American science into discipline-oriented societies. After the founding of the American Chemical Society, other discipline-oriented societies began to appear, including the APA. One can only speculate that the leaders of the AAAS must have felt grave concern over this development and feared consequences for the future of science if it did not remain unified—and perhaps they were right.

From the beginning, the unity sought by forming a national association for psychologists was challenged. Psychologists with applied interests, although few in number, were an awkward fit into the traditional academic structure of the APA. Membership in the APA was difficult to achieve; the values and priorities for applying psychology were not the same as those of the academicians, and the goals that those who applied or practiced psychology wanted to attain were foreign and sometimes objectionable to the academic members. The challenges in creating a unitary organization to include academicians, applied psychologists, and practitioners, challenges that still plague American psychology, were apparent from the earliest days, and grew more acute as the proportion of practitioners grew.

For most of its first 50 years, the APA primarily functioned as a learned society. The activities of the association were similar to the activities of other learned societies, such as those for philosophy, history, and anthropology. The members were primarily teachers, some of whom managed laboratories for their students and some of whom did original research. The leadership of the APA included some of the more prestigious members of the discipline. The presidency, a largely honorific position then, was a recognition of outstanding contributions to psychology. The APA included members who were concerned with professional practice, but the goals of practitioners received little attention or resources.

By the end of World War I, when large numbers of applied psychologists were ready to leave wartime service and join or return to the APA, the membership criteria were changed to make it all but impossible for nonacademic psychologists to attain membership. But the APA was faced with a serious conflict. To deny membership to the applied psychologists meant foregoing unity by ensuring the emergence of competitive psychological associations. As a compromise, a new, nonvoting category of *associate* was established for applied psychologists—a category that soon outnumbered members by three to one.

Far from preventing the emergence of other psychological organizations, this ambivalent solution may have actually encouraged spin-off organizations. Academic purists formed even purer organizations that excluded nonresearchers. Applied psychologists formed organizations to develop the profession of psychology, especially the rapidly growing American Association of Applied Psychology (AAAP). Public interest psychologists, frustrated with the APA's unwillingness to take a stand on social issues, founded the Society for the Psychological Study of Social Issues (SPSSI). Black psychologists felt better represented by their own organizations, the Black American Teachers Association; and women psychologists, who had little status in the APA, formed the National Council of Women Psychologists. For the first time, diverse and sometimes discordant voices spoke for American psychology, and the future of the APA as a unitary organization representing the entire range of psychology was in doubt. If the APA was to maintain its umbrella role, it would have to change to accommodate the diverse interests of psychologists. And change it did.

World War II was approaching and there was a need for psychologists, but some feared that psychologists, represented by so many different organizations, would not be able to work well together. The federal government played a significant role in the unification of psychology. The formation of the Emergency Committee for Psychology by the National Research Council, and the spirit of unity inspired by the impending war, led to efforts to bring together the diverse psychological organizations into a single association. In 1942, the emergency committee approved the convening of the Intersociety Constitutional Convention, representing nine national psychological societies. The APA, with 3,000 members, was much larger than all of the others combined, but although most of the members of the other organizations were also APA members, their agendas were different, and accommodating them required a new organization different from any of them.

The organization that grew out of the deliberations of the Intersociety Constitutional Committee retained the name APA for historical reasons, but it was so different that the chair, Edwin G. Boring, observed, "APA, while seeming to be continued in the proposed plan, would be so altered that it would be absorbed by the new organization" (Intersociety Constitutional Convention, 1943, p. 16).

The new APA was indeed a different organization. The statement of purpose was changed from the advancement of science to the advancement of psychology as a science, as a profession, and as a means of promoting human welfare. APA members became fellows, and associates became members—with full privileges. Some of the sections of the AAAP became divisions, the SPSSI became a division (Division 9), and a mechanism for establishing new divisions was provided. State and regional associations were eligible for affiliation, a council of representatives was established to broadly represent the membership and the employment of an executive secretary, and a full-time central office was approved. The new APA, designed to unify all psychologists, was inaugurated in 1945 (Hilgard, 1987, p. 757).

The reorganization of the APA led to a period of relative stability, but by the 1960s the increasing numbers of applied psychologists, and their growing influence in APA's governance, led to increasing dissatisfaction by academic psychologists and a strong desire on the part of many to reorganize the APA in a way that would provide more separation between scientific and applied psychologists.

Although reorganization had been discussed for years, the reorganization efforts of the late 1980s were the first to receive substantial attention by the Council of Representatives and to be placed before the members for a vote. Although there were many postmortem interpretations of why the majority of the APA membership voted to reject reorganization, the central issue may well have been the issue of unity versus fragmentation. Those who believed that the plan for a "new APA" made up of semiautonomous groups would further the fragmentation of the APA were not inclined to vote for it. Some of those who supported the plan did so in the belief that it would reduce friction among the main factions and thus avoid a formal split that might result in the demise of the APA as a unitary organization.

A good case could be made that both sides were right. Reorganizing the APA into a federation with a weak center and considerable independence for its constituent groups might well have created temporary peace while leading to a balkanization of the entire association into a collection of independent organizations with no coordination. Perhaps a more modest reorganization plan might have passed—but it might well have satisfied no one.

The prediction that failure to reorganize would lead to the formation of an alternative national organization for academic psychologists was confirmed, but the prediction that the new organization would draw most academics away from the APA was not. Even before the reorganization vote, some APA members had formed a group to plan for a new academically oriented association, and immediately after the vote they formed the American Psychological Society (APS). The goal of the APS leadership, which included a past executive officer of the APA and several APA past presidents, was to become the voice of scientific psychology and the new home for academic psychologists. The APA leadership believed that the APS's intent was to recruit the academic–research psychologists away from the APA, leaving the APA a practitioner organization and thus achieving full separation between scientific and applied psychologists and formalizing the split between science and practice.

For a variety of reasons, this did not happen. The APA engaged in active and successful efforts to retain members and recruit new ones. Although the APS attracted a substantial number of the APA's academic members, most of those retained their APA membership as well.

The APA continues to be the largest psychological organization and the only umbrella organization representing all kinds of psychologists, but there has been a great proliferation of organizations for various special interests and functions. In 1940, there were nine national psychological organizations. In 2003, there were more than 100 independent psychological organizations, although most of their members are also APA members. The proliferation of psychology organizations reflects the diversity of psychology and its activities, but cross-membership helps maintain organizational communication and cohesion.

In the view of some, the APA's efforts to be an umbrella organization that serves as both a learned society devoted to the advancement of the discipline and a professional association devoted to promoting the applications of the discipline has created an identity problem for the association. Learned societies exist primarily for information exchange among their members. Annual meetings are held for the presentation of scholarly papers and to give members the opportunity to meet colleagues to hold informal discussions. Journals are published to provided outlets for scholarly work, to extend the frontiers of the discipline and, indirectly, to advance the careers of members. Professional associations have an interest in preserving the *discipline*, but they are also concerned with promoting the *profession* and with self-regulatory activities such as ethics, licensing, and accreditation that characterize a profession. On the face of it, it is not easy for one organization to conduct both of these activities, and many believe the APA should focus on one or the other. However, circumstances have and continue to require the APA to act as both a learned society and professional association in both academic and applied contexts. The importance of training, regulatory, and legal issues, long matters of concern to the practice community, have now become significant issues within the academic community as well. Challenges from managed care and federal reporting requirements have raised the importance of a disciplinary identity within the practice and applied communities. The APA's experience in conducting *both* learned and guild activities provides a unique set of models.

Why is it important to have a unitary association representing the science and profession of psychology? Surely the advantages of a common voice in advocacy and in public image are apparent. During the past decade, the effectiveness of the APA's science advocacy has become the envy of many other scientific organizations. The APA has become a significant and responsible player in national policy decisions. More recently, the APA's professional advocacy has developed as a significant force at the national and state levels.

But there are more important reasons to keep a unified umbrella organization. In this diverse discipline, the APA remains the only overarching organization for psychology in which communication and information exchange takes place across a broad range of domains. It has achieved that role because the governance structure and the mechanisms for the APA to form policy or to act require that the many fragmented pieces interact. The history of the APA is the history of American psychology. The APA helped to establish the science of psychology by providing scientific conventions, by publishing the major psychological journals, and by preserving and disseminating the knowledge base. It also helped strengthen the status of the discipline by setting standards, creating rules, and defining best practices, across science and practice areas, and these vital roles continue to the present. Psychology has become one of the most successful scientific disciplines, and the APA has long been the leader among the world's national psychological associations.

While promoting and preserving scientific psychology, the APA has also helped to nourish and guide the development of the profession of psychology. In a few short years, professional psychology has moved from being a minor player to being one of the major health care disciplines. By providing strong professional and ethical standards and vigorously enforcing them, the APA has helped to make psychology a highly regarded profession as well.

THE AMERICAN PSYCHOLOGICAL ASSOCIATION AND FUTURE CHALLENGES TO UNITY

The pressures toward fragmentation, both conceptual and professional, that have characterized the evolution of psychology and of the APA are still very much alive today. National surveys indicate that a little more than 25% of all psychologists in the United States are employed in academic settings; 60% are service providers; and the remainder are employed in a wide variety of government, business, applied and research settings.[1] If the APA is to continue to represent psychologists in all of these settings, it is important to strengthen a sense of mutual goals and mission. The specter of failing to do so has led some to foresee a grim future for psychology: the exodus of scientists to other disciplines; the separation of professional training programs from scientific knowledge base and the profession from the science; and the balkanization of the strong national association into a number of smaller groups speaking for their special concerns but not for the entire discipline of psychology.

Avoiding such a grim prediction has been a concern of the APA for many years. This issue can be addressed organizationally in different ways. One is to actively promote interaction, respect, and unity within the discipline as part of a national agenda—at the convention, in dissemination media, through the encouragement of work on shared activities, and through books such as this one. The second is to recognize that there was probably no time in its history where psychology was sufficiently coherent in terms of approaches, theories, methods, or subject matter to have been called "one large family." A better metaphor might be to think of the discipline of psychology as a tribe, one in which there are many villages with intermarriage, divorce, conflict, and sometimes war but one that can nonetheless be identified as different from other tribes. In the case of psychology, this may be the discipline's understanding that its central phenomena take the individual organism as the most coherent unit and that its central concern is with how the organism–environment interaction is reflected in behavior, broadly defined. It is this focus that makes psychology different from the other disciplines, and that allows psychology to retain a core orientation in newly developing areas that combine with areas such as neuroscience, genetics, evolution, and community studies.

It is clear, however, that psychology as a discipline and the APA as an organization need to be proactive in promoting unity. This requires education, organization, and a view of the larger picture of the benefits to be gained from capitalizing on psychology's size and scope. Psychology needs to educate both the public and itself about its breadth, depth, and scope. Rather than offering disclaimers ("I am not really a psychologist—I am really a . . . cognitive scientist/human factors engineer/management expert/ neuroscientist/psychoanalyst (etc.)," we need to provide the tools to allow psychologists to offer examples of its broad reach and potential. Some of these tools are already available in the form of printed and electronic information about the applications of psychological research to solving

---

[1] APA Research Office.

pragmatic, socially relevant problems, but clearly more need to be developed and added to our educational and media campaigns.

The APA can also promote unity through organizational means, by harnessing the APA's broad convening powers to bring science and practice to the same table to address issues at the forefront of the national agenda: health disparities, the new media and technologies, preventing and responding to threat and terrorism, and so on. Indeed, it is the APA's breadth that makes it uniquely poised to integrate behavioral and social approaches to prevention and intervention, whether in health, education, or social welfare. Its broad convening power and the expertise represented by subject-matter expertise in close to 60 divisions position the APA to mount new kinds of transdisciplinary collaborations that allow those specialized in smaller sub-areas to interact and expand their impact.

In focusing on the challenges to unity, it is often easy to forget the opportunities available to the APA as the world's largest psychology organization and as one of the largest professional/science organizations. The APA's policy statements can create a mandate for the use of behavioral science knowledge in policy decisions; the APA's advocacy can influence legislative language to highlight the value and importance of behavior, behavioral science, and behavioral approaches to health, work, and education; the APA's considered issuance of guidelines, standards, and best practices can help set the bar for solid practice and application in both academic and applied settings.

REFERENCES

Bevan, W. (1982). A sermon of sorts in three plus parts. *American Psychologist, 37*, 1303–1322.

Bower, G. H. (1993). The fragmentation of psychology? *American Psychologist, 48*, 905–907.

Cattell, J. M. (1937). Retrospect: Psychology as a profession. *Journal of Consulting Psychology, 1*, 1–3.

Fowler, R. D. (1990). Psychology: The core discipline. *American Psychologist, 45*, 1–6.

Harrison, A. J. (1984). Science, engineering, and technology [Editorial]. *Science, 223*, 543.

Hilgard, E. R. (1987). *Psychology in America: A historical survey.* San Diego, CA: Harcourt Brace Jovanovich.

Intersociety Constitutional Convention. (1943, May 29–31). Condensed transcript. *American Psychological Association Papers (I-6/ICC 1943).* Washington, DC: Library of Congress Manuscript Division.

Kimble, G. A. (1984). Psychology's two cultures. *American Psychologist, 39,* 833–839.

Koch, S. (1959). *Psychology: A study of a science.* New York: McGraw-Hill.

Koch, S. (1969). Psychology cannot be a coherent science. *Psychology Today, 3,* 64–68.

Ladd, G. T. (1894). President's address before the New York meeting of the American Psychological Association. *Psychological Review, 1,* 1–21.

Roback, A. A. (1952). *History of American psychology.* Oxford: Library.

Staats, A. (1983). *Psychology's crisis of disunity: Philosophy and method for a unified science.* New York: Praeger.

5

SCIENTIFIC PSYCHOLOGY: SHOULD WE BURY IT OR PRAISE IT?

HOWARD GARDNER

Scholarly disciplines may seem immutable and immortal but in fact they exhibit a life course, sometimes smooth, sometimes not. A few disciplines, such as history, mathematics, and physics, set the gold standard: They have existed since classical times and remain a mainstay of secondary and higher education. Others, such as astrology, alchemy, or the study of bodily humors, disappear from serious consideration (although not, alas, from most bookstores). The medieval trivium of logic, grammar, and rhetoric still remains, but although logic has gained in importance within philosophy, neither grammar nor rhetoric are featured in most curricula. And still other disciplines, such as biology, have undergone a more complex course. On the one hand, biology has established strong ties to other subjects: biophysics, biochemistry, psychobiology. On the other, there are subspecialties—such as botany or genetics—that exist in almost separate spaces. Academic

In 1987 I gave an invited address to Division 1 of the American Psychological Association on the topic "Scientific Psychology: Should We Bury It or Praise It?" A version of this address was published in *New Ideas in Psychology* (1992). The invitation from Robert J. Sternberg to contribute to this volume has given me the opportunity to review and update my thoughts from 15 years ago. Revised and updated from *New Ideas in Psychology, 10*(2), "Scientific Psychology: Should We Bury It or Praise It?", 179–190, Copyright 1992, with permission from Elsevier.

institutions still need some way of classifying courses, allocating space, and taking votes, and so some collection of disciplines will necessarily endure. But whether the labels "biology," "music," "social studies," or "psychology" have a deeper coherence is a separate issue.

Dreams of a single unified psychology date back to the second half of the 19th century. William James wrote to his friend Thomas W. Ward, "Perhaps the time has come for psychology to begin to be a science" (quoted in Feinstein, 1984, p. 313). As he began to work on his classic textbook, James realized that the various parts of psychology did not yet cohere but he hoped that it would soon be possible to bridge the region "lying between the physical changes in the nerves and the appearance of consciousness in the shape of sense perceptions" (Feinstein, 1984, p. 313). Certainly there have been clear advances in many of the areas examined by James— the senses, emotions, attention, memory, reasoning, perception, and perhaps even James's beloved "stream of consciousness." Still, more than a century after the completion of *Principles of Psychology* it is germane to ask whether the field of psychology—with its many journals, associations, and lobbying groups—has also attained the status of a coherent discipline or domain.

At least on the level of lip service, the dream of a unified psychology continues. It can be sighted at the beginning and end of textbooks, although much less frequently in the intervening chapters. It surfaces as well in university catalogues. And occasionally a scholar will actually propose a formula or "central dogma" for the field—one that purports to link all the subfields (Cook, 1986). But for the most part, psychologists (like other academics) go about their daily teaching, research, and writing without agonizing about the actual or potential coherence of this field. In that sense, this book represents an anomaly, if perhaps a timely one.

Still, there are clear signs that a unified psychology remains elusive. The great surveyor of our field, Sigmund Koch (1981), became increasingly skeptical in his later years about the possibilities of a general psychology. Many other authorities have also expressed their skepticism (Baer, 1987; Bakan, 1987; Bickman & Goodstein, 1987; Krantz, 1987; Royce, 1987; Toulmin, 1987). Softer signs are equally alarming. Many universities have created hybrid fields such as cognitive science, brain and psychological science, cultural studies, human science, or (at my own university) "mind, brain, and behavior." And perhaps most revealing, it is becoming increasingly difficult to find the psychology section in any but the most scholarly of book stores. Academic bookstores are more likely to have areas such as cognitive science, general science, or social science. The ordinary book store abjures scientific psychology altogether in favor of human relations, sexuality, intimacy, and other "Dr. Phil-like" partitions of the field.

Inasmuch as psychology gives little convincing sign of cohering, we are faced with the following options.

1. We can simply close our minds to the possibility of disciplinary extinction and continue what we have been doing. No Super-body is likely to announce psychology as a fraud, and so we can maintain the status quo.

2. Following a well-known suggestion made with reference to the Vietnam War by the late senator George Aiken of Vermont, we can simply declare that psychology is a success—as it has been, according to many criteria—and swallow any lingering doubts that we might entertain.

3. We can hope that we are simply passing through a temporary phase of fragmentation and that some enterprising researcher or some brilliant theorist will discover the "golden thread" that will unify the field. In that context, the recent excitement around positive psychology (Seligman, 2002; Seligman & Csikszentmihalyi, 2000) offers one possible hint about how such a reconfiguration might come about. A unification around the methods and precepts of evolutionary psychology is another possibility (Pinker, 1997, 2002; Tooby & Cosmides, 1991). The very fact that the enthusiasts of positive psychology are unlikely to be equally enthusiastic about evolutionary psychology, or vice versa, must give one pause.

4. We can claim that there has been an unjustified romanticization of other disciplines. After all, there are any number of subfields of biology: the geneticists or molecular biologists inhabit quite different worlds from the evolutionists, taxonomists, or paleontologists. And economics is at least as top-heavy as psychology with schools that struggle against one another.

There are certainly other options, but I favor a fifth. Let us recognize that fields of science evolve, often in unsuspected and unexpected ways. Nearly every field begins as philosophy; and psychology continues to foreground its philosophical origins more faithfully than any other discipline. There was a period 200 years ago when psychology seemed impossible; a set of discoveries in the 19th century that established a number of enduring psychological paradigms and concepts, and a complex of social and historical factors in the 20th century earned psychology a place in virtually every academic environment (Boring, 1950).

Still, while psychology was developing, so were other fields of knowledge. It is against the background of other evolving disciplines that psychology must be understood and located. Earlier in the century, psychophysics—once the core of psychology—was slowly assimilated into engineering; and more recently, the study of animal behavior within psychology has been largely eclipsed by work from an ethological perspective. It is my contention that what we presently call psychology has already begun to be absorbed by a number of more fundamental disciplines, some more scientific (in the classical sense), some less so. The option that I favor is to discern psychology's place(s) within this emerging topography.

THE EMERGING DISCIPLINARY TOPOGRAPHY

Roughly paralleling breakthroughs in physics in the decades following the turn of the 20th century, and the parallel advances in molecular biology at mid-century, the years at the close of the 20th century can be well described as the coming-of-age of neuroscience. At every level of the nervous system, from the individual synapse to the blood-flow patterns through the entire cortex, knowledge is continuing to accumulate at a phenomenal rate. Those areas of psychology that were traditionally called physiological psychology and comparative psychology, as well as large portions of what are called sensation and perception, are rapidly becoming the concerns of neuroscientists. Indeed the topics of the first nine chapters of James's *Principles* (1890, 1963/1892; I refer hereafter to the shorter version [1963/1892] of that text) would all fit comfortably into a basic neuroscience course.

I should stress that I am not endorsing a reductionist position. The phenomena of sensation, perception, or other psychological states will never be reducible to "an account in terms of brain states." As is well indicated in the work of neurophysiologists such as David Hubel and Torsten Wiesel (Hubel, 1979), the categories and the level of psychological analysis will continue to be essential not only in ordinary discourse but also in the work of practicing neuroscientists. However, in my view, psychologically trained individuals will increasingly take their places as members of research teams that are probing the structure and functioning of the nervous system. The perceptual psychologist or psychophysicist working in isolation has become an anachronism.

If neuroscience will absorb much from the "lower regions" of psychology, an analogous kind of raid will be made by cognitive science—perhaps from the top, perhaps more laterally (Gardner, 1985). This recently emerging science is a self-styled interdisciplinary field that, like traditional psychology, seeks to uncover the basic processes of thought; however, adopting the current vogue, cognitive scientists regard the computer as the most suitable model for all forms of cognition. What changes is the *kind* of computer that serves as a model: In 1970 it was the serial von Neumann computer, whereas now massive parallel computation is foregrounded.

Although several disciplines are candidates for membership in an ultimate cognitive science, until this point scholars of psychology and artificial intelligence have been particularly central in cognitive–scientific endeavors. Many of the concepts and paradigms in cognitive science come from psychology, whereas the methods of research and other key concepts stem from computer science, especially artificial intelligence. Among contemporary areas of psychology, the fields of attention, memory, reasoning, problem solving, and the "higher forms" of perception and psychophysics are most closely affiliated with cognitive science. Parts of developmental, educational, and neuropsychology will fit comfortably under the cognitivist label as well. Most of the topics in the remaining chapters in James's briefer text (1963/1892), beginning with chapter 10 on habit and concluding with chapter 22 on reasoning, would also find a proper place in a text of cognitive science.

In the case of cognitive science, there is little danger of a reductionism that will exclude psychological analyses. (When neuroscience is included within cognitive science, it assumes a distinctly nonreductionist guise in that company.) A greater risk is that, in coming up with a core computational theory, researchers may shortchange those aspects of reasoning or problem-solving—for example, intuition—that are characteristic of humans rather than mechanical objects (Dreyfus, 1972). Also undetermined at present is the issue of whether the various subfields of cognitive science—for example, perception, attention, memory, reasoning—will prove any less unwieldy when thought of in computational terms than they were when conceptualized in traditional psychological frames. The ongoing dispute about the appropriateness of parallel-distributed processing models, as against von Neumann symbolic models, indicates that cognitive science may inherit psychology's woes (Pinker & Prince, 1988; Rumelhart & McClelland, 1986).

Neuroscience and cognitive science stand as the two behemoths, threatening to absorb many settlements of science, including the mainstream of research in psychology. When I surveyed the terrain 15 years ago, the hybrid "cognitive neuroscience" had just been coined. In an amazingly short period of time, cognitive neuroscience has become a major player in the research and teaching arena. Granting agents look to fund work in this cutting-edge area. Cognitive science seems less likely to be dominated by classical artificial intelligence models than to be swallowed by neural networks and connectionist models. And there is the perhaps inevitable sprouting of new subfields—developmental cognitive neuroscience and even social cognitive neuroscience. To be sure, fields such as social and developmental psychology are less likely to be swallowed in their entirety by cognitive neuroscience than, say, visual perception or long-term memory.

Still, I must voice my doubts about the scientific status of social psychology. I see social psychology as continuing to produce striking demonstrations about human social behavior—the kinds of findings associated in the past with researchers like Solomon Asch, Fritz Heider, Stanley Milgram, and Muzafer Sherif. As impressionistic and suggestive as these findings can be, I do not see them adding up cumulatively into a cohesive science. Indeed, my guess is that they are more likely to find their way into a general cultural discipline—including sociology, anthropology, and social psychology—than to be absorbed into more classical or aspiring sciences such as neuroscience or cognitive science.

During the time of my survey 15 years ago, I expressed the view that certain applied fields—such as educational, industrial, or clinical psychology—would continue to evolve without threat from cognitive neuroscience. At least in the case that I know best, educational psychology, this prediction was wide of the mark. Indeed, I have become quite deeply involved in a new concentration at the Harvard Graduate School of Education called "mind, brain, and education" (MBE). Proceeding centrally from the study of cognitive development (à la Jean Piaget and his successors), this new subdiscipline seeks to establish ties to brain science, on the one hand, and educational practice, on the other. Those of us in MBE are wary of the superficial applications to human learning of findings obtained from experiments with lower organisms. At the same time, we believe that genuine insights about learning and learning difficulties are emerging from the hard sciences and that these need to be understood by educators. Indeed, if educators are not knowledgeable about findings from brain science and genetics, decisions about formal education are increasingly likely to be made by physicians and basic scientists rather than by educators.

THE SURVIVING CENTER

It may seem that, in this Cook's tour of the disciplinary topography of the future, we have drifted far away from William James and his view of psychology. But that is only because I have yet to mention those subjects—and those chapters—that were central in William James's own account. I refer here to consciousness—treated in chapter 11; the self—treated in chapter 12; will—the concluding substantive chapter; and personality, which, although rarely mentioned explicitly by James, is in fact a looming presence in all of these chapters.

For James, the issue of the self or ego—its experiences, its internal and social aspects, its aspirations, and its evolution through life—is key in psychology. James lived in the pre-Freudian era but had already intuited some of the issues that were to occupy Sigmund Freud. And when he heard that Freud was coming to America, the ailing James made his way from Cambridge to Worcester and declared to the Viennese visitor, "The future of psychology belongs to your work." As historian H. Stuart Hughes once commented, "There is no more dramatic moment in the intellectual history of our time" (1961, p. 113).

Since the time of James and Freud, the study of personality, self, and will (hereinafter, the "person-centered trio") has occupied a paradoxical position within psychology. On the one hand these topics are clearly central in any delineation of the field, and they occupy predictably pivotal spots in textbooks. There are also classic textbooks on the topics, such as Hall and Lindzey's *Theories of Personality* (1978) and Ornstein's *The Psychology of Consciousness* (1986). And yet I must acknowledge there has been a slight embarrassment about these topics. While work continues on each of them, and many of the major figures in psychology have "had their say" on these topics, progress here is less compelling than in other strands of psychology. Indeed, in my view, with the exception of the path-breaking work begun in the late 1920s by Henry A. Murray (1938) and a few other significant contributors (Frijda, 1986; Lazarus, 1991; Plutchik, 1980), we have made relatively little progress in elucidating personality.

It is interesting to note that neither cognitive science, nor neuroscience, nor cultural studies has made much of a "grab" for these topics. I think this reluctance occurs not because these issues are difficult to study. I think it is because, rightly or wrongly, they are seen as central to psychology in a way that nothing else is—indeed they could be seen historically as the defining features of psychology. Notably, these topics seem particularly resistant to decomposition, elementarism, or other forms of reductionism— and of course, the cannibalizing disciplines exhibit strong tendencies in such atomistic directions. Perhaps equally interesting, this definition might well be shared even in remote cultures. Although failing to introspect about perceptual or cognitive processes, and displaying little interest in the study of other cultures or in stages of child development, preliterate societies do introspect and develop folk theories about the person and about personal experiences (Geertz, 1975).

If these fields are so central and yet have witnessed so little progress, what can we expect of them in the future? I think that we find a clue in the expansive psychologies of James, Freud, and Henry Murray. In one way or another, each of these scholars sensed an important truth: that the study of self or personality is at once a problem of psychology and a problem of literature. In the examples they use and in the approaches they adopt, each researcher has signaled the realization that the imaginative writer is tackling the same kinds of issues as the psychologist of personality. In James's case, of course, we have the lengthy and tortured relationship with his brother Henry as well as frequent references to other writers and to literary examples;

in Freud's case, there is his reliance on the great authors of the past—Sophocles, Shakespeare, Dostoevsky—for so many of his core concepts; in Murray's case, it is his deliberate appropriation of images from literature (e.g., "An American Icarus," in Murray, 1965) as well as his own pioneering scholarship on Herman Melville.

Literature constitutes an incredibly rich repository of information about human nature and personality, one that students interested in the person-centered trio ignore at their peril. It is not in the least surprising that the three scholars cited found particularly pivotal leads in the work of the great writers. But crucial insights about human nature are captured as well in other art forms, ranging from the visual arts to music to dance. The focus in this discussion falls on literature but the same line of analysis can—and should—be extended to other art forms.

But if there is a relationship between the scientific study of personality and the writer's investigation of the world of his or her characters, just what should that relationship be? Should it be mutual support and regular communication? Should the psychologist attempt to locate the novelist's characters in his or her laboratory? Should the novelist draw explicitly or implicitly on the psychological theories and concepts of the time? Or, to use a more contemporary conceit (Rorty, 1979), should the conversation occur among psychologists and literary critics and theorists? Should the methods developed by literary theorists be appropriated by psychologists to help them in studying the ways in which the individual (reader or writer) conceives of and relates his or her life? Should psychological insights about memory, sense of time, or identification be used by students of literature to explain the ways in which fiction works for different readers or is produced by different writers? Or are any or all of these options fair game (cf. Bruner, 1986, 1990, 2002)?

I remain uncertain just which form this collaboration will take, and perhaps several forms deserve exploration. At the very least psychological investigators of the person-centered trio ought to study works of art, including literature, with great care and test their portrayals against the claims of scientific study. Cooperative investigations among artists and psychologists could be profitable, although the difficulty of such collaborations should not be underestimated. Although the distance between psychologists and novelists might prove too great, psychologists and scholars of literature can each enrich one another's pursuits. Indeed, they may provide examples and "limiting cases" for one another, the psychologist's precise methods and rigor being balanced by the literary scholar's broad view and skeptical cast of mind. The psychologist's taxonomies and frameworks need to be tested against the rich range of characters found in literature and the powerful insights about the nature of text and of reading put forth recently by literary scholars. If the schemes of psychologists prove inadequate for dealing with these more rounded examples and concepts, then they need to be reconfigured or altogether scuttled. For their part, students of literature can benefit from a study of the way in which psychologists have conceptualized the human personality, operationalized these various conceptualizations, and tested certain tantalizing hypotheses about human behavior in the experimental laboratory (Holland, 1988).

It should prove possible for psychological writers and literary scholars to do more than read one another's publications. Here, indeed, I think that we can take an instructive leaf from colleagues in cognitive science and neuroscience. These fields have advanced in recent years in large measure because researchers reared in disparate disciplines work together shoulder to shoulder on problems of mutual interest. Topics such as the nature and appreciation of irony, the appeal of fairy tales, or the power relations obtain among individuals in Shakespearean plays have already benefited from cross-disciplinary investigations (Bettelheim, 1977; Brown & Gilman, 1989; Winner, 1988). Investigations at Harvard Project Zero (of which I am a member) have for some time benefited from these sustained collaborations among psychologists, artists, and experts in the systematic study of different art and literary forms (Gardner, 1982, 1990; Gardner & Perkins, 1989; Winner, 1982). The knottiest problems in artistic analysis—such as the question of whether there might be *the* correct interpretation of a work of art—call for interdisciplinary investigation.

Whatever collaboration eventually occurs among psychologists and individuals involved in literature and other art forms, one point seems clear. The part of psychology most likely to remain after the aforementioned cannibalizations have taken place is the study of the person-centered trio. Certain literary aspects of emotion and motivation may also elude the cognitive and neurosciences. These are topics for which psychologists may have special methods and insights; but they are equally the concern of writers and other artists and of those who study them, such as literary critics and theorists. No hard science à la physics is likely to emerge from the collaborations I envisage. But an interesting and highly useful kind of conversation between behavioral science and the humanities is likely to occur if psychologists and individuals in the arts make common cause. This insight was not lost on psychology's founders, and it has recently been reinforced in promising work undertaken by Donald Spence (1982) and Jerome Bruner (1986, 1990, 2002).

In the first version of this essay, I had spoken of a "personality quartet" rather than a "personality trio." The fourth member of the group was the area of human consciousness. Although the phenomenon of consciousness had been ignored in eras of behaviorism and early cognitive science, it has recently become a major growth industry in the psychological sciences. Just why this sudden explosion of interest has occurred is not easy to say. Probably it reflects a confluence of factors: the realization that a psychology (or human science) worthy of its name cannot afford to ignore a central aspect of human existence; the identification of neurological patients who exhibit certain forms of basic consciousness but not others (Weiskrantz, 1997); efforts to create neurological models of consciousness (Damasio, 1999; Edelman, 1992); an awakening of interest among philosophers, and especially among those with some grounding in the cognitive and neurosciences (Chalmers, 1997; Dennett, 1991; Searle, 1997). A paradox seems worth noting. On the one hand this energy has not come particularly from mainstream psychologists—and consciousness à la mode has yet to move centrally into textbooks (but see Baars, 1997). Yet on the other hand, nearly all those who are currently investigating consciousness recognize that it is a psychological problem and do not hesitate to draw on psychological findings and models. Perhaps consciousness—rather than personality, self, or will—will emerge as the topic around which the psychologically oriented sciences will ultimately coalesce.

WHITHER PSYCHOLOGISTS?

On his better days William James was a determined optimist, but he harbored his doubts about psychology. He once declared, "There is no such thing as a science of psychology," and added that "the whole present generation (of psychologists) is predestined to become unreadable old medieval lumber, as soon as the first genuine tracks of insight are made" (quoted in Allen, 1967, p. 315). I have indicated my belief that, a century later, James's less optimistic vision has materialized and that it may be time to bury scientific psychology, at least as a single coherent undertaking.

Yet scientific psychologists merit praise as well. If we have so far failed in our more ambitious undertaking, we have developed any number of paradigms, concepts, and methods that should prove serviceable in contemporary and future scientific endeavors. There is no need to chronicle these achievements, because they stock our textbooks and are now often common lore. Half a dozen psychologists have won the Nobel Prize in either economics or medicine/physiology; and there is now the prestigious Grawemeyer Award in Psychology, bestowed by the University of Louisville. If some psychologists suffer from "physics envy," I have no doubt that many in other disciplines experience "psychology envy."

We can rightly cherish the work of our most eminent practitioners—past and present—and the various concepts, findings, and schemes that they have developed. Whether psychology long endures as a self-contained field, scientists will long honor the discoveries of Donald Hebb and Karl

Lashley, the concepts of identity crisis and cognitive dissonance, the laboratory procedures of psychophysics, psycholinguistics, and physiological psychology.

Even as we pay homage to our past contributors, we can participate as full members of research teams in the emerging disciplines of cognitive science, neuroscience, and, perhaps, cultural studies and developmental studies. Individuals researching in these areas will need the insights and methods of psychology: And if our colleagues do not work with us, they will only have to repeat our mistakes and reinvent our fields.

A third point is perhaps more subtle but it is equally important. I think that the major contribution that psychologists can make is to continue to tackle the most interesting problems that emerge and to follow those problems wherever they may lead. To paraphrase an old saw, "Some scientists have avoided psychology because it is too easy; but others have avoided it because it is too hard." It is in our bones—as it was in the bones of William James—to pursue the hard issues; to display an audacious curiosity about the human condition, and to follow that curiosity wherever it looks.

One hundred and twenty-five years ago, William James's unstinting curiosity led him to physiology and thence to psychology—indeed to founding at Harvard around 1875 the first experimental laboratory in the country and perhaps in the world. The scientists who flocked to psychology in the 20th century are as gifted a lot of scholars as any I can imagine. Perhaps today, some of those who in an earlier era would have turned to philosophy or to psychology are instead attracted to computer science, brain science or genetics, to literature, or literary studies. Such shifting of allegiances is understandable and appropriate. But my guess is that a healthy number of the most curious will continue to gravitate to those vexed issues that, at least in their minds, are best described as being psychological in nature.

If one of those bright students were to wander into my office in search of career advice, what would I say? I would counsel the student to look for those issues, problems, and phenomena that seem to straddle the newly emerging fields. I would have in mind those problems that partake of cognitive science and neuroscience; that lie at the boundary of the individual self and the social self; that straddle stream of consciousness as a psychological concept and stream of consciousness as a presence in literature; that raise developmental issues in a neurological context or tackle neurological issues in a developmental vein; that occur at the interface of "pure cognition" and cognition as it unfolds in the school or at the working place. If psychology indeed turns out be a field for foxes rather than for hedgehogs—as I believe is the case—then I clearly would try to convert psychologists into the sleekest and cleverest foxes around.

CONCLUSION

In closing, then, I find myself taking a leaf from Marc Antony (or at least his literary incarnation). Having proposed a funeral for psychology as we know it, I have as well engaged in praise for much of what psychology has accomplished; and I have suggested that there is much productive work left for those who, for whatever reason, continue to call themselves psychologists and wish to pursue the kinds of issues and questions that are traditionally considered psychological. In so doing, I believe I have been faithful to the vision of William James, a man whose intellect was far too capacious ever to be corralled into a single discipline; and who in fact thrived by alighting on a topic for awhile and then moving on to another one—the proverbial fox, in Isaiah Berlin's figure. William James's long-time colleague Theodore Flournoy put it well:

> James' genius is so abundant, so varied, and so little preoccupied with the appearance of contradiction that in gathering in his various utterances, one does not easily frame him into a truly harmonious whole. Indeed it is almost a question whether he himself would have been able to produce a perfectly linked and coherent system from the magnificent treasure of material which he has left us. (Quoted in Allen, 1967, p. 495)

As psychologists in the second century of a post-Jamesian world, we could do worse than to emulate his spirit and his example.

REFERENCES

Allen, G. W. (1967). *William James*. New York: Viking.

Baars, B. (1997). *In the theater of consciousness*. New York: Oxford University Press.

Baer, D. M. (1987). Do we really want the unification of psychology? *New Ideas in Psychology, 5*, 355–360.

Bakan, D. (1987). Psychology's digressions. *New Ideas in Psychology, 5*, 347–350.

Bettelheim, B. (1977). *The uses of enchantment: The meaning and importance of fairy tales*. New York: Vintage.

Bickman, L., & Goodstein, L. (Eds.). (1987). Proceedings of the national conference on graduate education in psychology [Special issue]. *American Psychologist, 42*(12).

Boring, E. G. (1950). *A history of experimental psychology*. New York: Appleton-Century-Crofts.

Brown, R., & Gilman, A. (1989). *Politeness theory in Shakespeare's four major tragedies*. *Language in Society, 18*, 159–212.

Bruner, J. S. (1986). *Actual minds, possible worlds*. Cambridge, MA: Harvard University Press.

Bruner, J. S. (1990). *Acts of meaning*. Cambridge: Harvard University Press.

Bruner, J. S. (2002). *Making stories*. New York: Farrar, Straus, & Giroux.

Chalmers, D. (1997). *The conscious mind*. New York: Oxford University Press.

Cook, N. (1986). *The brain code*. London: Methuen.

Damasio, A. (1999). *The feeling of what happens*. New York: Harcourt.

Dennett, D. (1991). *Consciousness explained*. Boston: Little Brown

Dreyfus, H. (1972). *What computers can do: A critique of applied reasoning*. New York: Harper.

Edelman, G. (1992). *Bright air, brilliant fire*. New York: Basic Books.

Feinstein, H. (1984). *Becoming William James*. Ithaca, NY: Cornell University Press.

Frijda, N. (1986). *The emotions*. New York: Cambridge University Press.

Gardner, H. (1982). *Art, mind, and brain: A cognitive approach to creativity*. New York: Basic Books.

Gardner, H. (1985). *The mind's new science*. New York: Basic Books.

Gardner, H. (1990). *Art education and human development*. Los Angeles: Getty Center for Education in the Arts.

Gardner, H. (1992). Scientific psychology: Should we bury it or praise it? *New Ideas in Psychology, 10*(2), 179–190.

Gardner, H., & Perkins, D. (Eds.). (1989). *Art, mind, and education: Research from Project Zero*. Urbana: University of Illinois Press.

Geertz, C. (1975). On the nature of anthropological understanding. *American Scientist, 73*, 47–53.

Hall, C., & Lindzey, G. (1978). *Theories of personality*. New York: Wiley.

Holland, N. N. (1988). *The brain of Robert Frost: A cognitive approach to literature*. New York: Routledge.

Hubel, D. (1979). The brain. *Scientific American, 241*, 44–53.

Hughes, H. S. (1961). *Consciousness and society*. New York: Vintage.

James, W. (1890). *Principles of psychology*. Boston: Holt.

James, W. (1963). *Psychology: Briefer course*. New York: Fawcett. (Original work published 1892)

Koch, S. (1981). The nature and limits of psychological analysis. *American Psychologist, 3*(1), 257–269.

Krantz, D. L. (1987). Psychology's search for unity. *New Ideas in Psychology, 5*, 329–339.

Lazarus, R. (1991). *Emotions and adaptation*. New York: Oxford University Press.

Murray, H. A. (1938). *Explorations in personality*. New York: Oxford University Press.

Murray, H. A. (1965). An American Icarus. In G. Lindzey & C. Hall (Eds.), *Theories of personality* (pp. 162–175). New York: John Wiley & Sons.

Ornstein, R. (1986). *The psychology of consciousness*. New York: Penguin.

Pinker, S. (1997). *How the mind works*. New York: Norton.

Pinker, S. (2002). *The blank slate*. New York: Norton.

Pinker, S., & Prince, A. (1988). On language and connectionism: Analysis of a parallel distributed processing model of language acquisition. *Cognition, 28*, 73–193.

Plutchik, R. (1980). *Emotion: A psychoevolutionary synthesis*. New York: Harper & Row.

Rorty, R. (1979). *Philosophy and the mirror of nature*. Princeton, NJ: Princeton University Press.

Royce, J. R. (1987). More order than a telephone book. *New Ideas in Psychology, 5*(34), 1–345.

Rumelhart, D., & McClelland, D. (1986). *Parallel-distributed processing*. Cambridge, MA: MIT Press.

Searle, J. (1997). *The mystery of consciousness*. New York: New York Review Books.

Seligman, M. (2002). *Authentic happiness*. New York: Free Press.

Seligman, M., & Csikszentmihalyi, M. (Eds.). (2000). *American Psychologist on Positive Psychology* [Special issue], *55*.

Spence, D. (1982). *Narrative truth and historical truth: Meaning and interpretation in psychoanalysis*. New York: Norton.

Tooby, J., & Cosmides, L. (1991) The psychological foundations of culture. In J. H. Barkow, L. Cosmides, & J. Tooby (Eds.), *The adapted mind* (pp. 119–136). New York: Oxford University Press.

Toulmin, S. (1987). On not overunifying psychology. *New Ideas in Psychology, 5*, 351–353.

Weiskrantz, L. (1997). *Consciousness lost and found*. Oxford, England: Oxford University Press.

Winner, E. (1982). *Invented worlds: A psychology of the arts*. Cambridge, MA: Harvard University Press.

Winner, E. (1988). *The point of words: Children's understanding of metaphor and irony*. Cambridge, MA: Harvard University Press.

6

PARADIGM LOST, PARADIGM REGAINED: TOWARD UNITY IN PSYCHOLOGY

GREGORY A. KIMBLE

This chapter outlines a framework for unity in psychology. It maps out the territory in which the separate specialties of the discipline all have their own locations. In the words of Thomas Kuhn (1962), this map defines psychology's paradigm, the conceptual system that has served the discipline from its earliest beginnings. Despite the common gossip, there has been no

This article is a revised version of the author's Arthur W. Staats award address for unifying psychology, sponsored by the American Psychological Foundation and delivered at the 109th Annual Convention of the American Psychological Association on August 26, 2001.

I wrote this version of the chapter after spending about two months in the hospital with a mysterious ailment (possibly temporal arteritis, possibly anemia, possibly a stroke, possibly all of the above) that made it impossible for me to walk or even stand or sit alone because I had lost my equilibrium and sense of verticality. Therapy appears to be restoring these abilities but there are complications related to the role of overarching plans and more specific responses in the development of behavior. Although in my case the grand strategy for walking has always been there, the tiniest contributing skills—involving arms, legs, and toes as well as posture, trunk, and balance—exercise tyrannical control over it. Every one of them must fit into the general plan for progress to occur. A part of the solution to my problem has been at the level of cognition: Verbalizing or mentally rehearsing actions that I need to make turns out to help. Similar processes must complicate normal motor and cognitive growth. Accounts of such development that propose exclusively holistic or analytical approaches are surely incomplete.

paradigm shift in psychology. The version that proclaimed victory in the so-called cognitive revolution was actually the same old model dressed up to look politically correct.

Paradoxically, psychology has never recognized this ancient system as the basic fabric of its science. In this sense it is a paradigm lost. Unraveling that fabric exposes warps that are three categories of behavior and experience and wefts that are three axioms of action. This now-apparent structure is psychology's paradigm regained.

CATEGORIES OF BEHAVIOR AND EXPERIENCE

The categories of behavior and experience just referred to are the capabilities of knowing, feeling, and doing, identified in Plato's *Republic*. *Knowing* is what psychology calls cognition: such mental acts as thinking, reasoning, and problem solving. *Feeling* is the people's word for affect: such energizing forces as arousal, tension, and excitement. *Doing* has no standard psychological translation but *action tendency* has the needed connotations. It embraces active problem solving aptitudes as well as passive reflexes; it includes such dispositions as habit, response bias, and motor skill. Psychology uses these categories in the analysis and explanation of a host of psychological phenomena.

ANALYTICAL FUNCTION

Figure 6.1 presents examples of the analytical function, which depicts more elaborate processes as made up of the three fundamental components. Some of these analyses are explicit in the literature; others still await such recognition. Taking an example where the point is often missed, in proportions that vary from one person to another, an individual's self-concept is made up of so much self-knowledge (cognition), so much self-esteem (affect), and so much self-efficacy (action tendency). When that self breaks down in mental illness, the symptoms include irrational cognition, tormented affect, and deranged behavior. And as Paul Meehl (1996) once observed, effective treatment combines cognitive therapy (to correct disordered thinking), emotional therapy (to quiet troubled affect), and behavioral therapy (to cure unhealthy habits).

EXPLANATORY FUNCTION

The tripartite analysis in Figure 6.1 contains an implicit principle of synthesis. The arousal of one component evokes the others and they act

COGNITION	AFFECT	ACTION TENDENCY
Motivation [Also Instinct (McDougall, 1926)]		
Attention to Goal Objects	Arousal, Excitement	Goal-Seeking Behavior
Memory		
Memory for Information	Memory of Emotion	Memory of Action
Types of Intelligence		
Traditional IQ	Emotional Intelligence	Motor Skill
Self Concept		
Self Knowledge	Self Esteem	Self Efficacy
Traits of Personality (See Figure 6.4)		
Cognitive Style (Openness to Experience)	Affective Style (Positive-Negative Emotionality)	Reactive Style (Locus of Control)
Varieties of Temperament and Related Body Types (Sheldon, 1942)		
Cerebretonia (Ectomorphy)	Viscerotonia (Endomorphy)	Somatotonia (Mesomorphy)
Conflict		
Cognitive Dissonance	Conflict of Motives	Motor Conflict
Psychotherapy		
Cognitive Therapy	Emotional Therapy	Behavioral Therapy

Figure 6.1. Triarchic structure of psychological concepts. Sometimes, as in the cases of motivation, self-concept, and psychotherapy, psychology treats cognition, affect, and action tendencies as aspects of a single process. At other times, as with memory, intelligence, and conflict, they become different versions of a process.

together in the determination of psychological phenomena. Sometimes, as in common sense, psychology treats cognition, affect, and action tendencies as operating in that order. Looking at it this way, in the arousal of a fear, you see a bear (cognition), you are afraid (affect), you run (action tendency). But there are other possibilities. According to the James–Lange (1922) theory, the order is cognition—reaction tendency—affect: You see the bear, you run, and then you are afraid. Probably both of these sequences occur, but in individuals with different reactions to dangerous situations. For those with automatic habits that are available on such occasions, the James–Lange theory is correct: Motor acts occur before emotional reactions. But for those without prepared reactions, the emotion happens first. Usually the James–Lange order is more adaptive because, in situations of emergency, there is survival value in behavior that is faster than the relatively sluggish action of the autonomic nervous system.

AXIOMS OF ACTION

More than a century ago, Alfred Binet noted that a scientific explanation of psychological phenomena requires more than such a naming of their causes. It "consists in showing that each mental fact is . . . a particular case of [certain] general laws" (1883, p. 412). For Binet these laws were the structuralists' laws of association. Subsequent psychologists accepted Binet's conception but they proposed other fundamental laws. Examples from the teachings of the classical schools of psychology include the laws of conditioning for the behaviorists; perceptual organization for the Gestalt psychologists; and the survival value of behavior for the functionalists. Now, perhaps presumptuously, I nominate three different laws that have broad application—from the firing of a single neuron to the misfiring of a mind in madness. They are grounded in three separate realities.

POTENTIAL MADE MANIFEST BY INSTIGATION

The first of these realities is logical. As Aristotle noted, "[Any] coming-to-be necessarily implies the pre-existence of something which potentially 'is', but actually 'is not' " (*On Generation and Corruption*, bk. I, chap. 3). Aristotle's "coming-to-be" includes behavior and, translating this axiom into one that applies to psychology: The occurrence of a response, and its speed and vigor when it happens, are the consequences of potentials for and instigations to that action. *Potentials* are abiding attributes of organisms, the long-lasting cognitive, emotional, and motor strengths and weaknesses in which they vary. *Instigations* are more transient factors (signals, motives, inhibitors) that arouse potentials or suppress them.

ORIGINS OF BEHAVIOR

Genetics endows each of us with unrealized potentials for differences in such traits as intelligence (cognition), emotionality (affect), and athleticism (action tendency). Instigation, acting in specific situations during maturation and learning, decides the extent to which these potentials are realized and the circumstances under which they will be manifest. This thought is like the geneticists' concept of norm of reaction. Corresponding to every genotype (unrealized potential) there is a repertoire of phenotypes (realized potentials) that appear in different environments. As Figure 6.2 suggests, this way of looking at psychological concepts applies in contexts as remote from one another as neural impulses and mental illness. The format shown in Figure 6.2 depicts a causal chain that psychology assumes in many contexts, including

Instigation—Potential—Behavior
(Independent Variable) - (Intervening Variable) - (Dependent Variable)

(Norm of Reaction)
Environment - Genetic Potential - Realized Potential

(Nerve Conduction)
Stimulation - Resting Potential - Nerve Impulse

(Instinct Theory)
Releaser - Action-Specific Energy - Instinctive Behavior

(Sensory Thresholds)
Stimulus Intensity - Sensitivity - Reported Sensation

(Classical Theories of Learning)
Stimulation/Motivation/Inhibition - Habit - Performance

(Memory)
Cue - Memory Trace - Recall

(Psychopathology)
Stress - "Risk" for Mental Illness - Diagnosable "Disease"

Figure 6.2. Origins of behavior. In common theory, the remote causes of behavior are instigation and the immediate causes are potentials for behavior. Another way of putting it is that instigations, potentials, and measure of behavior are the independent, intervening, and dependent variables.

experimental procedures. Functioning as independent variables, instigations are the root causes of behavior. They give rise to proximate causes, potentials (sometimes called intervening variables), which are made manifest in dependent variables, indexes of action.

REALIZATION OF POTENTIAL

The realization of potentials comes about in three phases that Heinz Werner (1957) called an orthogenetic principle. Psychological development moves from undifferentiated and global operations, to more and more specific ones, and then to an integration of the differentiated components. Psychologists have observed this sequence in all of Plato's categories. William James described it for cognition, in his famous statement beginning with the observation that the baby, assailed by eye, ears, nose, skin, and entrails all at once, feels it as "one great blooming, buzzing confusion" (James, 1890, Vol. I, p. 488). My former Duke colleague, the late Katherine Banham Bridges (1932), proposed it for the unfolding of emotion out of generalized excitement, and C. E. Coghill (1929) observed it in the development of locomotion in salamanders.

An important by-product of this history is that, especially in early life, confusions may occur, both within and among cognition, affect, and reaction tendencies. In synesthesia, children sometimes mix up the details of sensory experience; for example, they may see numbers as having a certain hue. In psychoanalytical theory, the concept of primary process implies that children (and adults when they regress to childish thinking) confuse knowledge (cognition) with wishes (affect) and accomplishments (actions). The achievement of maturity requires the abandonment of such reactions.

The integration accomplished in the final stage of the orthogenetic sequence is hierarchical organization. Very general cognitive, affective, and action schemes control the operation of participating units. These schemata have what Karl Lashley (1951) called a "syntax of action," a concept that is easy to understand if you think of what you do in conversation. The idea you want to express establishes an unconscious strategy that decides the words and grammar that you use to make a sentence.

To develop this idea further: The thought you want to convey in any sentence initiates a strategy that takes the statement forward to a linguistically acceptable conclusion, unless something goes wrong—as happened in Bleuler's (1950) example of hebephrenic speech:

> Olive oil is an Arabian liquor-sauce which the Afghans, Moors and Moslems use in ostrich farming. The Indian plantain tree is the whiskey of the Parsees and Arabs. Barley, rice and sugar cane called artichoke, grow remarkably well in India. The Brahmins live in castes in Baluchistan. The Circassians occupy Manchuria and China. China is the Eldorado of the Pawnees. (p. 15)

Fragments of this utterance are locally coherent, suggesting underlying themes. Olive oil is associated with the Middle East; so are the Arabs, Afghans, Moors, and Muslims. Plantains, barley, rice, sugar cane, and artichokes are all food crops. The problem is that these themes lack organization. Even without psychopathology, the potential for such cognitive derailment occurs in everyone, and sometimes we all behave like schizophrenic patients. Although our sentences usually make sense, we speak words in a wrong order and commit occasional slips of the tongue.

INVOLUNTARY ACTION

An important ancillary principle is that, with practice, these integrated skills become increasingly automatic and unconscious. Once initiated, a well-learned habit moves to completion without conscious attention or deliberate intent. Usually such involuntary functioning serves a useful purpose. It frees the mind to deal with more important things. Every time you drive to work or school, you put yourself on automatic pilot and plan your schedule for the day. Irrelevant stimuli are excluded and inappropriate responses are suppressed. Sometimes, however, the process works against you—in two different ways.

First, the inhibited behavior may be exactly what is needed in a certain situation. On the Stroop test (Stroop, 1935) it is difficult to name the color in which a color name is printed if that color differs from the color name, because automatic reading habits frustrate the color-naming act. Or sometimes the excluded stimuli are the ones we should attend to. Driving automatically, our mind on other things (or busy with a cell-phone conversation), we fail to see a stop sign and cause an accident.

Second, conscious processing may evoke reactions that disrupt routines that are best left unconscious. Students understand that worrying about performance on a test can lead them to forget material they know well, And every college basketball player knows that attending to a free throw elicits thoughts and actions that can spoil a shot. The cure for this problem is additional practice and greater automaticity; missed free throws are less common in the National Basketball Association than in the college game.

It is important to understand that these automatic action tendencies are neither mandatory nor inevitable. They are default settings that control behavior unless they are overridden by the demands of situations. Thus, research participants actually succeed in naming the colors on the Stroop test, and more often than not, drivers detect impending danger and behave in ways that avoid accidents. Moreover, cognitive interference does not always lead to failure. Worriers often make As and even college basketball players make more than half their free throws.

ADAPTATION VERSUS COPING

The second reality is physical. Situations differ in two ways that have been important in the evolution of behavior.

First, objects vary in their effects on action tendencies. Some like food and praise are good—things that organisms strive to get more of. Others such as pain and ridicule are bad—things that organisms strive to get rid of. Ordinary people call these good and bad things rewards and punishments; they are also Thorndike's (1911) satisfiers and annoyers, Lewin's (1938) objects with positive and negative valence, and learning theory's positive and negative reinforcers.

Second, situations vary in the extent that they allow an individual to attain the good things and avoid the bad ones. Sometimes what a person does is ineffective: That look on mother's face means inevitable punishment—or unconditional love if the look is different—no matter what the child may do. More frequently, however, activities have consequences. Study harder and your course grades jump to A; stick with your present lazy habits and you get Bs and Cs—or worse.

The evolutionary consequences of these contingencies are two different ways of dealing with the realities that created them: active coping in situations organisms can control and passive adaptation in those they cannot control. Aristotle made that same distinction in what he called the "active and passive affections of the soul" (*De Anima*, bk. I, chap. 4), noting that "teaching is the activity of a person who can teach [but] the operation is performed on some patient" (*Physics*, bk. III, chap. 3) and that "a man who is a doctor might [also] cure himself" (*Physics*, bk. I, chap. 9). Adaptation changes organisms in ways that meet the requirements of an unyielding environment; coping changes the environment to satisfy the needs of organisms struggling for survival.

ADAPTATION AND COPING IN SEVERAL CONTEXTS

Adaptation and coping are adjustments possessed by every living creature but, with evolution, the balance between them became increasingly weighted on the side of coping. The behavior of plants is almost entirely adaptation. Darwin (1859) described it in some detail in his discussions of the twining stems of climbing vines, the twisting trunks of trees, and the gravity-sensitive growth of the roots of plants, all of which promote survival by maximizing the light and nourishment that plants receive. Darwin was also fascinated by the one variety of botanical coping that he knew about: the behavior of the insect-eating plants. But coping is predominantly an animal adjustment. Because of its survival value it becomes increasingly dominant as one ascends the phylogenetic ladder.

The neural basis for the distinction between adaptation and coping is already evident in the nervous system of infant animals, in a sequence that begins with coping.

> Early in development, internally generated spontaneous activity [coping] sculpts circuits on the basis of the brain's "best guesses" at the initial configurations of connections necessary for function and survival. With maturation . . . the developing brain relies less on spontaneous activity and increasingly [adapts in ways the depend] on sensory experience. (Katz & Shatz, 1996, p. 1133)

A familiar application to behavior of this way of thinking occurs in Jean Piaget's (e.g., 1973) distinction between assimilation and accommodation. *Assimilation*, like coping, is a process of interpreting (sometimes distorting)

In Processes That Are Primarily Cognition
Bottom-Up Versus Top-Down Perceptual Processing
Perceiving Versus Conceiving Problem Solving
Receptive Versus Expressive Aphasia
Mindless Versus Mindful Learning (Langer, 2000)

In Processes That Are Primarily Affect
Fear Versus Avoidance
Passive Aggression Versus Acting Out
Obsession Versus Compulsion
Extrinsic Versus Intrinsic Motivation

In Processes That Are Primarily Action Tendency
Classical Versus Instrumental Conditioning
External Versus Internal Locus of Control
Learned Helplessness Versus Learned Competence
Automatic Versus Intentional Action

Figure 6.3. Adaptation and coping in cognition, affect, and action tendency. Although as the term *versus* implies, psychology often sees adaptation and coping as mutually exclusive alternatives, they actually are not. Behavior is a blend of these processes, just as it is a blend of the underlying components, cognition, affect, and action tendencies.

information in terms of available mental organizations. *Accommodation*, like adaptation, changes mental systems so that they become a better match to the outside world. Newborn infants cope by sucking breasts—or a finger or a blanket if one is placed on their lips. Fingers and blankets are not breasts, however, and the infant accommodates, first by changing lips and mouth and, eventually, by ceasing to suck such objects.

Figure 6.3 shows adaptation and coping in contexts that primarily entail cognition, affect, and action tendency—where psychology tends to see them waging war with one another. You will understand, however, that adaptation and coping work together and that behavior reflects a blending of their influences. They operate on all of Plato's dispositions and appear in bad as well as good adjustments. An obsessive–compulsive patient with claustrophobia shows passive adaptation in the obsessive knowledge (cognition) that enclosed places bring on fear (affect) and active coping in the compulsive habit (action tendency) of avoiding such locations. A successful academic knows (cognition) and values (affect) scholarship—both adaptation—and works in the library or the laboratory (action tendency) to make a contribution—thus, coping with the problem of gaining recognition in the community of scholars, not to mention tenure.

ROLE OF EXPERIENCE

The exploitation of these mechanisms as ways of dealing with controllable and uncontrollable events depends on experience. Organisms cannot know about such actualities until they have experienced them. For organisms that exist today, important aspects of this experience is in evolutionary history. Some happenings in the world, such as day and night, and spring, summer, fall, and winter, occur in cycles. The contemporary consequences of these uncontrollable periodicities are numerous diurnal rhythms, winter hibernation, and the seasonal affective disorders—all forms of adaptation, some of them more adaptive than others. Presumably the same evolutionary history accounts for such inborn coping patterns as defense of territory, mate selection, and predation.

In human living, years of contact with these controllable and uncontrollable realities produce dimensions of adjustment that are anchored by coping and adaptation, for example those that range from suspiciousness to trust, dominance to submission, and obstinacy to obedience. Moreover, continued exercise makes these habits automatic and involuntary. They become "functionally autonomous" (Allport, 1937); they happen without external instigation. They resemble motives and find a place in some psychologists' lists of secondary drives.

OPPONENT-PROCESS THEORY

The third reality is physiological. Behavior is under the simultaneous control of excitation and inhibition, even in the synaptic transmission of neural impulses. Without making the physiological connection, Aristotle noted that "if there be a movement natural to the soul, there must be a counter-movement to it, and conversely" (De Anima, bk. I, chap. 3). In 1686, Sir Isaac Newton advanced the same idea as his third law of motion, noting that "To every action there is always opposed an equal reaction: or, the mutual reactions of two bodies upon each other are always equal, and directed to contrary parts" (quoted in Cajori, 1947, p. 13).

EXCITATION AND INHIBITION IN CONTEXT

As Aristotle's reference to movement and countermovement implies, these opponent processes are slaves to one another. Excitation elicits inhibition and inhibition elicits excitation—in all of Plato's categories.

In cognition—for example, in the cocktail party situation—attention to one conversation (excitation) excludes (inhibits) others. The excluded conversations are somehow there, however. Your attention turns instantly to a different one if someone drops your name. In 1890, William James noted that "nature implants contrary impulses to act on many classes of things" (Vol. 2, p. 292), and suggested that "inhibition is a vera causa, of that there can be no doubt" (Vol. 1, p. 167). He recognized that inhibition operates in mental as well as physical activities, appearing, for example, as satiated meaning: "If [you] look at an isolated printed word and repeat it long enough. . . . it stares at [you] from the paper like a glass eye, with no speculation in it" (Vol. 1, p. 181).

For affect, Solomon and Corbit (1970) explained the time-course of emotion, using excitation and inhibition as these processes operate in visual afterimages. They introduced their theory with this example: A woman's fear, created by her doctor's report that she has breast cancer, quickly rises to a maximum and then subsides a little. Later on, when she learns that the lump in her breast is a nonmalignant cyst, her response is euphoria, rather than emotional neutrality as might be expected when the reason for her worry disappears. Opponent-process theory explains that sequence this way: The diagnosis of a breast cancer excites fear, and fear evokes an inhibiting process that is the opposite of fear. Although this inhibiting process remains unconscious, inhibited itself by fear, it gradually gains strength. At first, excitation is totally dominant and the woman is in a state of panic. But, with time, increasing inhibition decreases her fear slightly. When the news about the nonmalignant cyst removes the fearful stimulus, only the opposite of fear remains, and her emotion is the negative afterimage of fear—euphoria instead of an emotional gray.

For action tendencies, Sherrington (1906) viewed the entire nervous system as operating on a system of excitatory and inhibitory checks and balances. For example, the patellar reflex could not occur if some muscles were not inhibited at the same time as opposing muscles were excited. William James took a similar position but he put the point more dramatically: "We should all be cataleptics and never stop a muscular contraction once begun, were it not that other processes simultaneously going on inhibit the contraction" (1890, Vol. II, p. 583).

In posttraumatic stress disorders, all of these reactions come together. Cognitively, patients show the effects of excitation in "flashbulb" memories and other thoughts that interfere with ongoing functions; they show inhibition in cloudy consciousness and the repression of traumatic experiences. In the area of affect, excitation takes the form of irritability, aggression, and other intense emotional reactions that are irrelevant to the situation; inhibition becomes emotional numbness and loss of the joy of living. In the case of action tendencies, excitation may produce excessive alertness and tense expectancy, whereas inhibition creates fatigue and nonresponsive apathy (Selye, 1976).

CONCEPT OF THRESHOLD

One incidental implication of this opponent-process law is that it accounts for the concept of threshold, sometimes treated as a first principle of behavior (Kimble, 1996). What scientists call "thresholds" reflects the situation that exists when the strength of excitation is just enough greater than the strength of inhibition to allow an action to occur. In the sensory processes, the absolute threshold is the strength of stimulation that elicits a tendency to respond positively (excitation) that is barely greater than the counter-urge (inhibition) to avoid producing "false alarms." In the diasthesis–stress (threshold) theory of psychopathology, maladaptive behavior occurs when internal and external stress breaks though the inhibitory control that normally restrains them.

THEORY OF PERSONALITY

To show a larger application of the ideas just presented, I now put them all together in a theory of personality (Figure 6.4). Although it was acceptable in my generation for experimental psychologists to know about such things, I am not a personality theorist. Figure 6.4 just shows how my notions play out in what I take to be that context. Read the figure from top to bottom. Environmental causes, modified by the physiology of excitation and inhibition, operate on genetic potentials that correspond to cognition, affect, and action tendencies to create analogous realized potentials. The most general of these derived potentials are three fundamental traits of personality: openness to experience, positive–negative emotionality, and locus of control. In obedience to Werner's orthogenetic law, these global traits differentiate into more specific ones—some opposites, some personal strengths, some weaknesses—and then come together in a more or less coherent integration that allows them all to live together in a single tenement of clay. With instigation, these traits find expression in behavioral manifestations that allow psychology to know them.

CONCLUSION

This application to personality completes my presentation of psychology's recovered paradigm. As I have noted resurrecting it, this model dates back more than 2,000 years. Plato's writings set the stage for treating behavior as a reflection of cognition, affect, and action tendencies, and my three axioms of action are all in Aristotle. Distinguished pedigrees are not enough to guarantee the viability of ideas, however, and over time developments

ENVIRONMENTAL CAUSES
Positive/Negative Reinforcers
Controllable/Uncontrollable Environment

X

BIOLOGICAL CAUSES
Excitation/Inhibition

Operate on Three Genetic Potentials

COGNITION	AFFECT	ACTION TENDENCY
(innate intellect)	(energy level)	(approach-avoidance)

To Produce Three General Traits of Personality
(General Realized Potentials)

COGNITIVE STYLE	EMOTIONAL STYLE	REACTIVE STYLE
Openness to Experience	Positive-Negative Affect	Locus of Control
(Perceiving-Judging)	(Optimism-Pessimism)	(Field-Body Orientation)

Which Differentiate Into More Specific Traits
(All of Them Dimensions)

SELF-KNOWLEDGE	SELF-ESTEEM	SELF-CONTROL
CREATIVITY	MOODINESS	WILLFULNESS
SENSATION SEEKING	SOCIABILITY	IMPULSIVENESS
SOPHISTICATION	NEUROTICISM	PERSEVERENCE

And Achieve an Organization that Creates an Integrated Individual

With Instigation, Traits Give Rise to Behavioral Expressions
That Make Them Knowable

Figure 6.4. A theory of personality implied by the ideas explicit in this theory, environmental causes, modified by excitation and inhibition, operate on genetic cognitive, affective, and action tendency potentials to create realized potentials, including the fundamental traits of personality: openness to experience, positive–negative emotionality, and locus of control. These global traits differentiate into more specific ones and then acquire an integration. With instigation, they become manifest in behavior.

in science forced psychology to modify its outlook. The most significant adjustment was the insistence on public observability as the hallmark of scientific knowledge. This criterion forces the (often reluctant) recognition that if psychology wants to be a science it must, at bottom, be some form of behaviorism because the only public facts available are organisms' responses and the situations that evoke them.

But the form that psychology takes is not necessarily classical behaviorism. Once it accepts the obligation of factual accountability for its statements, psychology can be as cognitive, physiological, or humanistic as it chooses, provided only that the cognitive, physiological, or humanistic concepts it uses have operational definitions that refer them to situations and behavior. Disciplines that study similar topics—the mind, the brain, or human potential—without those connections are sometimes science, sometimes not, but they are not psychology. With that understanding, this recovered paradigm—which I once called functional behaviorism (Kimble, 1996) because of its attention to the adaptive quality of behavior and its ties to evolution—does good things for our discipline.

First, it expands the horizons of psychology. It legitimates the study of mental processes—even going by their street names, which some other versions of behaviorism banish from the field.

Second, it provides psychology with two essential components of a science: categories of understanding—cognition, affect, and action tendency —and fundamental laws—potential–instigation, adaptation–coping, excitation–inhibition—that have extensive application.

Third, it demonstrates that relationships among these laws and categories can clarify such conceptions as personality that are difficult to understand, or even to describe, because of their complexity.

Fourth, it unifies psychology by giving the various specialties (experimental, biological, clinical, and the rest) identifiable locations in a larger scheme of things. It makes equal partners of Cronbach's (1957) two scientific disciplines of psychology—experimental psychology, which relates behavior to situations, and psychometric psychology, which predicts behavior from other behavior, for example on a test.

Fifth, it resolves a number of long-standing controversies in psychology.

- It brings peace to the nature–nurture battle with the insight that behavior is an expression of genetic potentials that are realized in ways that depend on environmental instigation.
- It settles the mind–body argument by making mind and body symbiotic components of a single science in which both participants suggest processes for the other one to look for. The resulting discoveries—in the environment or beneath the skins of organisms—add credibility to both approaches.
- It puts into perspective the major sticking point that separates holistic from atomistic views of behavior and experience, both of which turn out to be correct, depending on the slice of life examined and the level of analysis.
- It eradicates the fault lines that separate psychology's diverse cultures—scientists from humanists, empiricists from rational-

ists, behaviorists from mentalists, theorizers from experimenters, and academics from practitioners (Kimble, 1984)—by showing that they all share the goal of seeking understandings of behavior.

REFERENCES

Allport, G. W. (1937). *Personality: A psychological interpretation.* New York: Holt, Rinehart & Winston.

Binet, A. (1883). *Du raisonment dans les perceptions. Revue Philosophique, 15,* 406–432.

Bleuler, E. (1950). *Dementia praecox or the group of schizophrenias.* New York: International Universities Press.

Bridges, K. M. B. (1932). Emotional development in early infancy. *Journal of General Psychology, 49,* 229–240.

Cajori, F. (Ed.). (1947). *Sir Isaac Newton's mathematical principles of natural philosophy and his system of the world.* Berkeley: University of California Press.

Coghill, C. E. (1929). *Anatomy and the problem of behavior.* New York: Macmillan.

Cronbach, L. J. (1957). The two disciplines of scientific psychology. *American Psychologist, 12,* 671–684.

Darwin, C. (1859). *On the origin of species by means of natural selection.* New York: D. Appleton.

James, W., & Lange, C. G. (1922). *The emotions* (K. Dunlap, Ed.). Baltimore: Williams & Wilkins.

Katz, L. C., & Shatz, C. J. (1996). Synaptic activity and the construction of cortical circuits. *Science, 274,* 1133–1138.

Kimble, G. A. (1984). Psychology's two cultures. *American Psychologist, 39,* 833–839.

Kimble G. A. (1996). *Psychology: The hope of a science.* Cambridge, MA: MIT Press.

Kuhn, T. S. (1962). *The structure of scientific revolutions.* Chicago: University of Chicago Press.

Langer, E. J. (2000). Mindful learning. *Current directions in psychological science, 9,* 220–223.

Lashley, K. S. (1951). The problem of the serial organization of behavior. In L. A. Jeffress (Ed.), *Cerebral mechanisms in behavior: The Hixon symposium* (pp. 112–146). New York: Wiley.

Lewin, K. (1938). *Contributions to psychological theory: The conceptual representation of psychological forces.* Durham, NC: Duke University Press.

McDougall, W. (1926). *An introduction to social psychology.* Boston: Bruce Humphries.

Meehl, P. E. (1996, August). *Credentialed persons, credentialed knowledge.* Paper presented at the 104th annual convention of the American Psychological Association, Toronto, Ontario, Canada.

Piaget, J. (1973). States of cognitive development. In R. I. Evans (Ed.), *Jean Piaget: The man and his ideas* (pp. 105–175). New York: E. P. Dutton.

Selye, H. (1976). *The stress of life* (Rev. ed.). New York: McGraw-Hill.

Sheldon, W. H. (1942). *The varieties of temperament: A psychology of constitutional differences.* New York: Harper & Row.

Sherrington, C. S. (1906). *The integrative action of the nervous system.* London: Constable.

Solomon, R. L., & Corbit, J. D. (1974). An opponent–process theory of motivation: I. Temporal dynamics of affect. *Psychological Review, 81,* 119–145.

Stroop, J. R. (1935). Studies of interference in serial verbal reactions. *Journal of Experimental Psychology, 18,* 643–662.

Thorndike, E. L. (1911). *Animal intelligence.* New York: Macmillan.

Werner, H. (1957). *Comparative psychology of mental development.* New York: Knopf.

7

UNIFICATION OF PROFESSIONAL PSYCHOLOGY THROUGH SOCIAL RELEVANCE

RONALD F. LEVANT

Sternberg (2003) has called for the unification of psychology, putting this forth as the central initiative of his presidency of the American Psychological Association (APA). He offered some good reasons to unify psychology, including (a) conserving scarce resources, (b) enhancing psychology's credibility with policy makers, and (c) improving cohesion among psychologists.

As previous chapters in this volume have discussed, psychology is a diverse discipline and profession, with many subspecialties. In turn, many of these subspecialties of psychology are rife with factors that would impede unification, such as competing theories, methodologies, and outright schisms. For example, my field of gender studies seemingly put to rest the ancient debates between essentialism and social constructionism, only to see them reemerge with evolutionary psychology's recent rise.

How, then, does one unify psychology? What overarching theme would be sufficiently compelling to unite all of psychology's disparate "tribes"? For periods of time in the history of the discipline, certain paradigms have swept the field and provided at least a semblance of unification. Psychoanalysis, humanism, behaviorism, and cognitivism all had their day of preeminence.

Yet psychologists have always had clashes of these paradigms, as reflected in famous debates, such as the one between Skinner and Rogers or the one between Snygg and Meehl (Shlien, 1970).

Sternberg and Grigorenko offered a framework for the unification of scientific psychology, which requires that one takes a much broader view of the phenomena under investigation and work toward a "multiparadigmatic, multidisciplinary, and integrated study of psychology" (2001, p. 1069).

This chapter will discuss the unification of professional psychology. I want to begin by quoting from a recent presentation from former APA president Ronald Fox:

> The real tragedy of psychology's failed promise as a profession is . . . that we know so little about how to help our fellow man and are poorly positioned to apply what we know. We should be more concerned with how to prevent war, how to deal with poverty, how to cope with racism, and the reduction of human misery and suffering than with the truly petty questions that clog the arteries of too many of our scholarly deliberations. Wresting with the big issues and large-scale solutions gives professions their significance and purpose. (2003, p. 1)

I want to advance the argument that for professional psychology to fulfill its promise, it must grapple with the big issues, namely society's most pressing problems. Society, of course, demands that psychology (like other learned professions) respond to its most pressing needs, and directs the flow of resources to those psychologists and other professionals who are most relevant to its perceived needs. On the other hand, those professionals and professions who ignore society's pressing needs are at risk for extinction.

It is my hope that we can create a consensus that meeting society's most important needs should be the mission of professional psychology. If we are successful, we will have unified professional psychology around the overarching theme of societal relevance.

From my current positions as both a dean of a graduate school of psychology and an officer of the American Psychological Association (APA), I have a unique vantage point from which to both observe and reflect on the process whereby professional psychology responds to urgent societal needs, and how these needs thus influence the evolution of professional psychology. As I see it, as a result of societal needs for psychological knowledge and service, the scope of psychological practice is expanding and diversifying into new areas, areas where the distinction between applied scientist and professional practitioner is blurred. The new areas I am referring to include health psychology (and its related aspects such as psychology in primary care, psychoneuroimmunology, and applied psychophysiology), and also neuropsychology, rehabilitation psychology, forensic psychology, child and family psychology, multicultural psychology, geropsychology, business and industry consultation, and psychopharmacology. I think that, as a result of psychology responding to social needs, the future evolution of professional psychology will entail the development of roles that do not now exist or are just emerging—in health care, the public sector care, the courts, the correctional system, schools, businesses, and so forth—in the numbers that psychologists entered the role of outpatient therapist in the 1970s and 1980s. In this chapter, I illustrate this process by discussing four areas of professional practice that are evolving in response to societal needs: psychological health care, psychopharmacology, serious mental illness, and promoting resilience in response to war and terrorism.

PSYCHOLOGICAL HEALTH CARE

We are truly living in interesting times. The 21st century promises monumental changes in health care, education, communication, and science in general. The technology currently available has already provided the tools whereby educated consumers can make critical decisions regarding their own health care and health care providers can call up databases (such as Epocrates®) to provide up-to-date information on pharmaceutical agents. Yet despite these promising developments, the status of health care in the United States is worrisome.

Health care costs have once again begun to escalate faster than other segments of the economy, and uninsured individuals number more than 43 million Americans. In June 2002, the secretary of the Department of Health and Human Services (HHS) met with leaders from the National Academies and challenged them to propose bold ideas that might change conventional thinking about the most serious problems facing the health care system today. The Institute of Medicine (IOM) reported,

> The American health care system is confronting a crisis. . . . Tens of thousands die from medical errors each year, and many more are injured. Quality problems, including under-use of beneficial services and overuse of medically unnecessary procedures, are widespread. And disturbing racial and ethnic disparities in access to and use of services call into question fundamental values of equality and justice for all. *The health care delivery system is incapable of meeting the present, let alone the future needs of the American public.* (emphasis added; 2002, p. 1)

These problems beg for the active involvement of U.S. health care professionals, who are the most educated group in society and who therefore (in my view) have an affirmative duty to use their knowledge for the betterment of society. Psychology is clearly part of this group, and psychology has broad applicability to health care (Newman & Vincent, 1996).

One of the most important issues in psychology today is the redefinition of some parts of the profession[1] from specialty mental health care to primary health care. As a specialty profession of mental health care, we deal primarily with the people who self-identify as having psychological problems and who have access to a mental health specialist. This is just a fraction of those who need psychological services. As a primary health care profession we would be able to serve the much larger group of people who do not have access to mental health care or who do not identify their problem as psychological. To grasp this potential, please consider a few facts about health care:

1. Seven of the top health risk factors are behavioral (tobacco use, alcohol abuse, poor diet, injuries, suicide, violence, and unsafe sex; VandenBos, DeLeon, & Belar, 1991).

2. Seven of the nine leading causes of death have significant behavioral components (McGinnes & Foege, 1993).

3. At least 50% (and maybe as much as 75%) of all visits to primary care medical personnel are for problems with a psychological origin (including those who present with frank mental health problems and those who somaticize) or for problems with a psychological component (including those with unhealthy lifestyle habits such as smoking, those with chronic illnesses, and those with medical compliance issues; Campbell et al., 2000).

4. Stated another way, one study found that fewer than 16% of somatic complaints had an identifiable organic cause (Kroenke & Mangelsdorff, 1989).

5. A large number of studies have demonstrated that providing behavioral health care reduces the use of medical and surgical care (Chiles, Lambert, & Hatch, 1999; Sobel, 1994).

6. The vast majority of people receiving mental health treatment are cared for by medical professionals with minimal specific training in mental health.

7. Moreover, there is a growing body of empirical evidence supporting the effectiveness of psychological interventions in ameliorating a wide range of physical health problems, including both acute and chronic disease affecting literally every organ system and encompassing pediatric, adult, and geriatric populations. In addition to being clinically effective, these interventions are dramatically less expensive than alternative somatic interventions across a wide variety of illnesses and

---

[1] Some professional areas would clearly remain specialty care—for example, neuropsychology.

disorders, including cardiovascular disease, hypertension, diabetes, neoplasms, and traumatic brain injury (Freidman, Sobel, Myers, Caudill, & Benson, 1995; Groth-Marnat & Edkins, 1996; Smith, Kendall, & Keefe, 2002).

Descartes's 17th-century philosophy, which separates mental health from physical health, is finally loosening its hold, and as a result psychology has a tremendous opportunity to evolve into a premier primary health care profession. At the very least this should put psychologists on the front lines of health care, working collaboratively with physicians and nurses. The more visionary perspective is that health care should be reorganized so that psychologists serve as primary caregivers at the gateway to the health care system, functioning to diagnose and treat the more prevalent psychological problems and referring to medical physicians when indicated.

What do psychologists who function in the physical health care arena actually do? I asked that question of one of my colleagues, Professor Jan Faust of Nova Southeastern University, who is a pediatric psychologist. Her response follows:

- psychological intervention for adjustment to the diagnosis, treatment, and prognosis of serious illness (pediatric cancer, HIV-AIDS, hemophilia etc.);
- preparation for anxiety-provoking and painful medical procedures including surgery;
- ameliorating needle and blood phobia and difficulties swallowing pills;
- reduction of anticipatory nausea and vomiting;
- pain management for burns, bone marrow aspirations, and spinal taps;
- facilitating medical adherence for diabetes, asthma, and other diseases with complex medical regimens;
- helping adolescents and their families make medical decisions such as terminating life support, choosing experimental chemotherapy protocols, and amputation. Addressing the aftermath of these decisions;
- preventing pediatric intensive care unit psychosis—altering patterns in living to prevent psychotic symptoms as a response to disrupted circadian rhythms;
- neuropsychological assessment for accidental injuries (car and bike accidents);
- emergency room intervention with those patients in crisis;
- end-stage counseling and grief work for terminally ill children and their families;
- developing failure-to-thrive eating protocols;
- treating obesity, anorexia, and bulimia;
- therapy for children who have disfiguring, dysmorphic, and debilitating conditions, including neurological impairment;
- treating urinary and fecal incontinence;

- educating medical personnel on psychosocial issues;
- enhancing communication between medical personnel and among medical personnel, patients, and their families;
- reducing burnout of medical personnel; and
- helping medical personnel with their grief when losing patients.

All of this suggests a huge potential market for psychological services in health care systems. To access these opportunities, however, psychology must define itself as a health profession rather than as a mental health profession. In fact, an APA Board of Professional Affairs Work Group has called for a "figure-ground reversal" in professional psychology (APA, 2000). That is, rather than viewing itself as a mental health profession with health psychology representing a subset of its expertise, the group advocated a view of psychology as a health profession, with mental health as a subset of its expertise. Such a change in perspective would require a rather dramatic change in training programs.

A serious limitation on psychologists' ability to participate in integrated health care has been the absence of payment mechanisms to reimburse psychological services within general health care settings. Psychologists have not been permitted to bill under procedure codes such as evaluation and management of medical disorders, patient education, and preventative services. As a consequence, they were forced to bill under mental health codes, which are often inappropriate, or to make arrangements with care systems to bundle their services. Moreover, psychologists did not have easy access to reimbursement for services provided to patients related to nonpsychiatric diagnoses, even when these services are well accepted clinically and are strongly supported by the empirical literature. However, the recent approval of the Center for Medicaid and Medicare Services of the Health and Behavior codes for psychologists may well be the vehicle to address these problems. This allows psychologists to see patients for medical diagnoses in their private offices and bill for assessment and intervention.

In conclusion, I believe that, because of societal and economic pressures, behavioral health will be integrated into the health care system and that this development is as inevitable as the industrialization of health care was 15 years ago. The only question is what position will psychologists occupy in the coming integrated health care system? Will we be replaced by primary care MDs and subdoctoral personnel or will we emerge as a premier health profession? It is up to us!

THE PRESCRIPTIVE AUTHORITY INITIATIVE

The prescription privilege agenda has the capacity to dramatically accelerate the evolution of professional psychology and to move the field closer to fulfilling its potential of being a top-tier health care profession. The Department of Defense (DoD) Psychopharmacology Demonstration Project graduates who are now prescribing have demonstrated through the U.S. Government Accounting Office (1999) and Vector Research (1996) reports that not only will properly trained prescribing psychologists *not* be a public health hazard, as psychiatry has claimed for so many years, but also that such psychologists will do an outstanding job at psychodiagnosis and at expertly combining psychological and pharmacological treatment (Sammons & Brown, 1997; Sammons & Levant, 1999). This is what has been called the psychological model of prescribing. Morgan Sammons (personal communication, January 15, 1999), a prescribing psychologist in the U.S. Navy, indicated to me that many of his patients come to him on many different psychoactive drugs (given the current penchant for polypharmacy) and that he carefully takes them off medications to see how they are functioning and how they will respond to psychotherapy. He then may add back medication as needed.

The major argument for psychologists prescribing is that it would improve public health (Levant & Sammons, 2002). As I noted earlier, most people with a mental health or substance abuse problem are receiving psychoactive drugs that are prescribed by a primary care prescribing professional who has minimal training in mental health, which does not augur well for their being able to conduct the first prerequisite for prescribing— namely, making an accurate diagnosis. And the data suggest that they do not: Such professionals miss the diagnosis of depression more than half of the time, and they undertreat it when they do catch it. And it is even worse with substance abuse disorders. Clinical psychologists obtain more training in the identification of mental disorders and illnesses than any other health care practitioners, including psychiatrists. Hence, appropriately trained prescribing psychologists will increase the public's access to comprehensive mental health care.

Equally powerful is the continuity-of-care argument and the fact that outcome research has demonstrated that the most effective treatment for many mental health disorders is a combination of psychotherapy and medication. Allowing appropriately trained psychologists to prescribe medication will result in increased continuity, integration, and quality of patient care. Patients who are treated by prescribing psychologists will need to see only one doctor for all of their mental health treatment and will be spared the expense, burden, and inefficiencies of seeing a psychiatrist or primary care physician solely for the purpose of receiving medications.

There is also the argument of precedent. Many non-MD health professionals currently prescribe safely (e.g., osteopaths, podiatrists, dentists, advanced nurse practitioners, optometrists, physician assistants), and their services are highly beneficial to the public. Throughout the course of the

20th century, a number of health professions have successfully sought to better serve patients by expanding their scope of practice to include prescription privileges, and organized medicine has reflexively and automatically opposed any threat to what was once their monopoly over the prescription pad. Early in the 20th century, it was dentists, osteopaths, and podiatrists who found themselves at odds with organized medicine. All can now independently prescribe medications to their patients. For the past 25 years, optometrists, nurse practitioners, physician's assistants, and psychologists have faced the same obstacles. Optometrists now have some form of prescriptive authority in all states, nurse practitioners in all states, physician assistants in 46 states, and, as mentioned earlier, the U.S. DoD now allows properly trained military psychologists to prescribe. Fortunately, the only thing as constant as organized medicine's warnings about impending disaster if one profession or another is granted prescription privileges is the consistency with which state legislatures have batted away these arguments.

One question that often arises is, How can the public be assured that the psychologist who is prescribing their medications is properly trained? The APA undertook extraordinary measures to ensure patient safety. A Blue Ribbon Panel, composed of nationally recognized health professionals and scientists with expertise in medicine, psychiatry, nursing, pharmacy, neuroscience, psychology, and public policy developed a rigorous and comprehensive model curriculum for psychologists who wish to receive training to prescribe psychotropic medications (California Blue Ribbon Panel, 1995). In addition, an independent body was commissioned to create a thorough examination in psychopharmacology that effectively measures the knowledge needed for safe prescribing. We anticipate this exam being used by states as one criterion for ensuring that only psychologists with proper academic and supervised training experiences are granted prescriptive authority.

Most states do not have statutes granting prescriptive authority to psychologists. The question arises: Why should psychologists undertake this training now? The short answer is that they should undertake the training to provide the best possible care to their patients. Because so many patients of psychology these days are taking psychoactive medications (and this number is growing, especially with kids), we are probably doing a disservice to clients if we do not make some efforts to fully understand how medications work and when they might be indicated and contraindicated. We need to have the knowledge necessary to understand and evaluate the appropriateness of all aspects of patients' treatment. Because most patients are getting their prescriptions from nonpsychiatrists, there is also a huge role to be played by appropriately trained psychologists in advance of the passage of a law as consultative psychopharmacologists. Although this role has been challenged recently in several jurisdictions (Massachusetts, Florida, and

Washington, DC), the Board of Psychology in all three instances has upheld this role as part of psychologists' scope of practice. This role now has statutory authority in California with the passage of S.B. 983 in 1998. Moreover, overwhelmingly graduates of postdoctoral training programs have said that this training has had an enormous impact on their practice. They get more referrals, particularly from medical physicians, their access to hospital practice is increased, their testimony in court is more highly valued and sought, and in every other conceivable way their practices have been enhanced.

What is happening across the country? Today there are 11 programs offering postdoctoral training in psychopharmacology. It was estimated that more than 900 psychologists have pursued or are pursuing such training. As of March 2004, 330 graduates of such training programs requested application materials for the new examination in psychopharmacology offered by the APA Practice Organization's College of Professional Psychology, and 63 have been admitted to exam. (The pass/fail rate for the exam is not yet public.)

Legislatively, 31 state psychological associations have committees focusing on prescriptive authority, and bills have been introduced in 13 states. The Social Health Index developed by the Fordham Institute for Innovations in Social Policy (Miringoff, Miringoff, & Opdycke, 2001) indicates that almost all of these states are ranked in the bottom half of the Social Health Index.

In 1993 the Indiana Psychology Code was rewritten to include the following provision: "Nothing in this article shall be construed as permitting a psychologist to prescribe medication, unless a psychologist is participating in a federal government sponsored training or treatment program."

On December 30, 1998, in the last hours of the session, the Guam legislature overrode a governor's veto, making B. 695 public law, which now states: "Section 121204. *Prescriptive Authority*. A clinical psychologist may administer, prescribe, and dispense any licensed drug as a delegated authority of the Collaborative Practice Agreement (CPA). . . ."

And of course there is the startling success of the New Mexico Psychological Association. They very nearly got a prescriptive authority bill passed in 2001 and, of course, became the first state to authorize appropriately trained psychologist to prescribe psychoactive medication on May 6, 2002.

FORDHAM SOCIAL HEALTH INDEX

The success of the prescriptive authority initiative has also had a visible impact on the profession in at least two major ways. First, wherever I travel I am told that this initiative is a morale builder, coming at the end of a long period of great demoralization because of the excesses of managed care. It builds morale because it is viewed as expanding the scope of practice and facilitating psychologists' roles in primary care and serving the underserved. Second, those psychologists who have undertaken the training report tremendous enhancements to their ability to practice, whether they are prescribing psychologists in the U.S. military or civilian psychologists who function as consultative psychopharmacologists in either the public or private sector.

PSYCHOLOGISTS AND SERIOUS MENTAL ILLNESS

When the topic of psychology becoming a primary health care profession is discussed, sometimes it is also implied, if not stated outright, that psychologists should leave behind the role of specialty mental health care profession. Although I strongly support the move into primary care, I also want to make a strong case for retaining psychology's role in mental health care. That is, I want to put forward a "both/and" position, but with a twist. Both initiatives would involve an expansion of the professional role with the aim of making psychology the premier behavioral health care profession. Both roles would also require significant change in how psychologists now practice.

We need to deepen psychology's involvement in specialty mental health care, particularly where it is needed most—namely, in the care of those suffering from serious mental illnesses. Outside of the VA system, psychology does not currently play a major role in the treatment of individuals with serious mental illnesses, such as schizophrenia and other psychotic disorders, and is not an important presence in the public sector systems that provide most of the care that goes to seriously mentally ill patients. Although clinical psychology once specifically defined its purview as serious psychopathology, this area has largely been abandoned to psychiatrists and subdoctoral personnel. This is somewhat ironic. It is also short-sighted because in this era of cost-containment and shrinking opportunities for the practice of psychology, the care of such patients represents a potential growth area, one based on an expanded scope of practice.

The Center for Mental Health Services (CMHS, 1996), part of the U.S. Substance Abuse and Mental Health Services Administration, estimates that 5.4 million adults (2.7% of the population) have a "severe and persistent" mental illness, and that more than 3 million children and adolescents have a serious emotional disturbance that undermines their present functioning and endangers their future.

As most would agree, this large and vulnerable population receives substandard care. Deinstitutionalization, which was conceived in the human-itarianism and the idealism of the community mental health movement of the 1960s, has been a stark failure overall (although there have been some success stories here and there). With the clarity of 20/20 hindsight, we can see that there was insufficient investment in community-based care and psychological rehabilitation to make it work. There was also an overreliance on psychoactive medications, which (again in retrospect) was terribly short-sighted, given the lack of adequate care systems designed to prevent relapses because of noncompliance. In the end, the deinstitutionalization movement succeeded in emptying the beds of the state mental hospitals and filling the streets and jails with chronic mental patients. Indeed, an article in the *New York Times* described the jail as the "new mental hospital" (Butterfield, 1998).

Having worked with people who suffer from serious mental illnesses off and on over many years, I have found that many have complex comorbidities, including (in addition to their serious mental illness) substance abuse, brain injury, posttraumatic stress disorder (PTSD, particularly among the women, many of whom have been victims of rape), and *DSM–IV* Axis II (American Psychiatric Association, 1994) diagnoses such as borderline personality disor-der (to name some of the more common diagnoses). Also, because of the harsh lifestyle of the street of many members of this population, there are often untreated medical problems as well. A population this vulnerable and disabled deserves much better care than society now offers.

Psychologists could play a significant role in the care of this population. Some in the mental health field promote the idea that serious mental illness is a "brain disease" and therefore treatable only by biological interventions (e.g., medications). Furthermore, the outcome research literature strongly indicates that although psychoactive medications can suppress the symptoms of serious mental illness, psychological rehabilitation actually holds out hope for recovery (Anthony, 1993; Coursey, Alford, & Safarjan, 1997).

The concept of recovery is really quite an important notion in that it confronts the stigmatizing stereotypes that view serious mental illness as essentially hopeless. Too often such long-term conditions as schizophrenia and bipolar disorder (to name just two) are viewed extremely pessimistically, as incurable conditions. But evidence has been accumulating that indicates that people diagnosed with serious mental illness do recover through a combination of psychotherapy, psychosocial rehabilitation, consumer-run self-help programs, and medications. The concept of "recovery" in this work involves a shift in perspective from a medical to a rehabilitative model.

We must continue to work to change public policies and social attitudes that regard these illnesses as hopeless and thereby allow the disgraceful neglect of people who suffer from them to continue. The APA has begun this process with the passage of the Resolution on Stigma and Serious Mental Illness by the APA Council of Representatives in February 1999.

Hence, I think that we have a lot to offer in the care and treatment of the seriously mentally ill patient. First, there is no profession better qualified than psychology to conduct the careful diagnostic assessments that would tease out the complex comorbidities from which many of these individuals suffer. Second, because psychologists have taken the lead in developing and evaluating psychological rehabilitation and recovery methods, we can surely lay claim to the role of designing, implementing, and training staff members to carry out psychological rehabilitation. Third, we can provide empirically validated therapies for people with serious mental illness. Fourth, practitioners can team up with researchers and develop the next generation of psychological interventions that might have even greater effectiveness (Bellak, Mueser, Gingerich, & Agresta, 1997; Dixon & Lehman, 1995; Linehan, Armstrong, Suarez, Allmon, & Heard, 1991). Fifth, we can play a larger role in the medical aspects of these patients' lives. Ultimately, of course, we could prescribe psychoactive medications after the successful passage of prescription privilege legislation. Right now psychologists with the appropriate postdoctoral training and supervised experience can function as consultative psychopharmacologists, who, working in conjunction with primary care physicians or in some states even nurse practitioners, can provide the full spectrum of care for the seriously mentally ill patient. Psychologists' role as consultative psychopharmacologists for the seriously and persistently mentally ill population has been delineated by an APA Board of Educational Affairs Task Force on consultative psychopharmacology.

Sixth, such an enhanced role in the care of seriously mentally ill people would go a long way toward furthering the aim of becoming the premier primary behavioral health care profession. By reaching out and responding effectively to a public health problem of this size and scope, we would surely establish credibility. Furthermore, such an expanded role is consistent with other efforts to expand the scope of practice of psychology in areas such as health care, brain injury, and the courts.

The critical factor is going to be the development of new pathways to practice. In the care for the seriously mentally ill patient, new pathways to practice are clearly needed, based on an expanded scope of practice as outlined earlier. Some universities are now offering training in this area (e.g., Nova Southeastern University, Boston University, University of Maryland), but much more needs to be done. The field needs postdoctoral retraining programs that include training in psychological rehabilitation and consultative psychopharmacology, legislation to change archaic civil service staffing patterns where they still exist, and entrepreneurship to develop psychological delivery systems in those states that outsource mental health care.

Psychology would also be well advised to work to develop partnerships with recovered patients. There is a growing cadre of people who have recovered from serious mental illness who can serve as invaluable allies in the recovery process. Many of these "consumers," also known as "survivors of psychiatric treatment" and "ex-mental patients," are interested in collaborating with psychologists and deeply believe from their own experiences that psychotherapy and psychosocial rehabilitation can be beneficial. But to develop such a coalition, these consumers state clearly that psychologists must understand their perspectives on such matters as participating in their own recovery, the integration of self-help with professional services, living with a diagnosis of serious mental illness, forced treatment and its alternatives, and the abuses that many have experienced in the mental health system (Bassman, 1997; Freese & Davis, 1997).

PROMOTING RESILIENCE IN RESPONSE TO WAR AND TERRORISM

Surprisingly, people in therapy reported no difference in their stress levels once the war with Iraq started. But that may be only because war was seen as just one more stressor in chronically stressful times, according to a new survey of psychologists by the APA Practice Directorate. The survey, conducted with "real-time" reporting by psychologists both before and after the first bombs of the war fell (March 20–24, 2003), was mailed to 446 psychologists, and 225 were returned (51% response rate). They found that psychologists said that 67% of patients were affected by the threat of war and 42% discussed war and the threat of terrorism in their most recent session. In addition, although only one patient initiated therapy because of concerns about current events, 13% of patients already in treatment were concerned enough about war and terrorism for it to become a focus of their treatment, according to the psychologists who responded to the survey. Psychologists surveyed also reported that the threat of war and terrorism had an emotional impact on many patients' lives: 28% of patients felt that the greatest emotional response was apprehension; nearly 19% of patients felt distress; and nearly 18% felt anger.

Of course, the attacks of September 11th did much to create this sense of chronic stress and anxiety. As we know, the intent of terrorism is precisely to create this state of anxiety. To the extent that psychology can contribute to enhancing the resilience of citizens so that people react with less anxiety, we reduce not only the impact of terrorism but also the incentives for terrorists to engage in violent acts. Hence, there is a need for good information on psychological resilience and programs designed to help citizens deal with the continuing threats of terrorism.

The APA, the American Psychological Foundation, and Verizon, Inc., have provided funding for the APA Task Force on Promoting Resilience in Response to Terrorism. The task force is developing information that is most likely to help citizens deal with the stress, anxiety, and fear caused by terrorism. The work product will present a range of information in the form of fact sheets designed for professionals who work with different groups in society: children, adults, older adults, people of color, first responders, people suffering from serious mental illness, and so forth.

To provide a scientific foundation for this effort, the task force reviewed the literature on psychological resilience, as well as the literature on terrorism in other countries (e.g., Northern Ireland, Israel) and on the response to natural disasters such as hurricanes and earthquakes. However, it is clear that natural disasters are different from terrorism, because they lack the element of intentionally inflicting harm on innocent and defenseless civilians that many find so abhorrently cruel. The literature suggests that several variables are associated with postdisaster psychological status. Predisaster psychological vulnerability (e.g., earlier episodes of PTSD), degree of exposure to the traumatic event during and immediately after the disaster, and the occurrence of major life stressors (e.g., loss of home, unemployment) are associated with poorer postdisaster adjustment. On the other hand, personality resources such as resilience or hardiness and social support are associated with better postdisaster psychological status. Stress inoculation programs and programs for dealing with acute and chronic stress and anxiety are likely to be of significant help in coping with the threat of terrorist attack. However different segments of a diverse society have different methods of coping and managing stress. Hence we need to keep the diverse needs of a pluralistic society uppermost in mind as we develop this information. Recent data suggest that age and gender are associated with the development of PTSD following the September 11 attacks, with children and females more likely to develop symptoms. Also of interest, those who watched greater amounts of television depicting the attacks were more likely to develop symptoms. Little is known about how specific ethnic groups respond to disasters and hence more research is needed in this area. One challenge for the future is to design and evaluate psychoeducational programs aimed at enhancing the factors of resilience (confident optimism, productive and autonomous activity, interpersonal warmth and insight, and skilled expressiveness) and hardiness (a sense of control over one's life, commitment as a result of finding meaning in one's existence, and viewing change as challenge; Levant, Barbanel, & DeLeon, 2003).

WHAT CAN PSYCHOLOGISTS DO?

Psychologists who have expertise in any area that might help address the threat and impact of terrorism and war are encouraged to direct their attention toward these problems. Psychologists who do not have training in the area of disaster response might consider obtaining such training and then becoming part of the APA Disaster Response Network. Psychologists with expertise in the area of promoting resilience might consider offering continuing education workshops to their colleagues and also working with their state and local psychological associations to offer resilience enhancement programs in their local communities. In addition, the APA began its "Road to Resilience" campaign after September 11, 2001, to teach resilience skills and has added to that with its "Resilience in a Time of War" series of brochures as a result of the war with Iraq.[2]

We are at the proverbial fork in the road as a society in dealing with this problem. There are many ways that psychologists can help, and we have sketched just a few of them. The stakes are high. If we can help, we must.

CONCLUSION

In this chapter I discussed new pathways, responsive to societal needs, for the evolution of professional psychology in such areas as psychological health care, psychopharmacology, the public sector care of seriously mentally ill individuals, and promoting resilience in response to war and terrorism. There are of course many other pathways that I did not talk about such as opportunities in business and industry, the media, the schools, the courts and correctional system, communities of faith, and in the public policy process. However, I think the take-home message of my chapter should be this: Fewer than 5% of the population have doctoral degrees. Hence, we are among the most highly educated people of this time. As a result we have an affirmative duty to use this knowledge for the betterment of society. Psychology is applicable to every aspect of human life. As former APA president Patrick DeLeon has said, if we take care of society's most pressing needs, society will take care of us. The future of this profession will be unified and as bright as we dare to imagine.

---

[2]These materials, including brochures aimed at consumers; parents and teachers of very young children, parents and teachers of elementary school children, parents and teachers of middle-school children, parents and teachers of high schoolers, and teenagers are available by calling toll-free 1-800-964-2000 or by free download at www.helping.apa.org

REFERENCES

American Psychiatric Association. (1994). *Diagnostic and statistical manual of mental disorders* (4th ed.). Washington, DC: Author.

American Psychological Association. (2000). *Report of the Board of Professional Affairs Work Group on expanding the role of psychology in the health care delivery system.* Washington, DC: Author.

Anthony, W. A. (1993). Recovery from mental illness: The guiding vision of mental health service system in the 1990s. *Psychosocial Rehabilitation Journal,* 16(4), 11–23.

Bassman, R. (1997). The mental health system: Experiences from both sides of the locked doors. *Professional Psychology: Research and Practice, 28,* 238–242.

Bellack, A. S., Mueser, K. E., Gingerich, S. G., & Agresta, J. (1997). *Social skills training for schizophrenia.* New York: Guilford Press.

Butterfield, F. (1998, March 5). By default jails become mental institutions. *New York Times,* pp. A1, A13.

California Blue Ribbon Panel. (1995). *Final report of the California Blue Ribbon Panel.* Sacramento, CA: Author.

Campbell, T. L., Franks, P., Fiscella, K., McDaniel, S. H., Zwanziger, J., Mooney, C., et al. (2000). Do physicians who diagnose more mental disorders generate lower health care costs? *Journal of Family Practice, 49,* 305–310.

Center for Mental Health Services. (1996). *Mental health, United States, 1996* (R. Manderscheid & M. Sonnenschein, Eds.) (DHHS Publication No. SMA 96-3098). Washington, DC: U.S. Government Printing Office.

Chiles, J. A., Lambert, M. J., & Hatch, A. L. (1999). The impact of psychological interventions on medical cost offset: A meta-analytic review. *Clinical Psychology: Science and Practice, 6,* 204–220

Coursey, R. D., Alford, J., & Safarjan, W. (1997). Significant advances in understanding and treating serious mental illness. *Professional Psychology: Research and Practice, 28,* 205–216.

Dixon, L. B., & Lehman, A. F. (1995). Family interventions for schizophrenia. *Schizophrenia Bulletin, 21,* 631–643.

Fox, R. E. (2003, August). *Toward creating a real profession of psychology.* Paper presented at the annual convention of the American Psychological Association, Toronto, Ontario, Canada.

Freese, F. J., & Davis, W. W. (1997). The consumer/survivor movement, recovery and consumer professionals. *Professional Psychology: Research and Practice, 28,* 243–245.

Friedman, R., Sobel, D., Myers, P., Caudill, M., & Benson, H. (1995). Behavioral medicine, clinical health psychology, and cost offset. *Health Psychology, 14,* 509–518.

Groth-Marnat, G., & Edkins, G. (1996). Professional psychologists in general health care settings: A review of the financial efficacy of direct treatment interventions. *Professional Psychology: Research and Practice, 27,* 161–174.

Institute of Medicine. (2002). *Fostering rapid advances in health care: Learning from system demonstrations.* Washington, DC: Author.

Kroenke, K., & Mangelsdorff, D. (1989). Common symptoms in ambulatory care: Incidence, evaluation, therapy, and outcome. *American Journal of Medicine, 86,* 262–266.

Levant, R. F., Barbanel, L. H., & DeLeon, P. H. (2003). Psychology's response to terrorism. In F. Moghaddam & A. J. Marsella (Eds.), *Understanding terrorism: Psychological roots, consequences, and interventions* (pp. 265–282). Washington, DC: American Psychological Association.

Levant, R. F., & Sammons, M. T. (2002). Towards evidence based training and practice in psychopharmacology: Of cassandras, canards, and the dog in the night-time. *Clinical Psychology: Science and Practice, 9,* 259–263.

Linehan, M. M., Armstrong, H. E., Suarez, A., Allmon, D., & Heard, H. L. (1991). Cognitive–behavioral treatment of chronically parasuicidal borderline patients. *Archives of General Psychiatry, 48,* 1060–1064

McGinnis, J. M., & Foege, W. H. (1993). Actual causes of death in the United States. *Journal of the American Medical Association, 270,* 2207–2212.

Miringoff, M., Miringoff, M.-L., & Opdycke, S. (2001). *The social health of the states.* Tarrytown, NY: Fordham Institute for Innovations in Social Policy.

Newman, R., & Vincent, T. (1996). Balancing expertise with practical realities. In R. P. Lorion, I. Iscoe, P. H. DeLeon, & G. R. VandenBos (Eds.), *Psychology and public policy: Balancing public service and professional need* (pp. 203–206). Washington, DC: American Psychological Association.

Sammons, M. T., & Brown, A. B. (1997). The Department of Defense psychopharmacology demonstration project: An evolving program for postdoctoral education in psychology. *Professional Psychology: Research and Practice, 28,* 107–112.

Sammons, M., & Levant, R. (1999). Combined psychosocial and pharmacological treatments: Introduction. *Journal of Clinical Psychology in Medical Settings, 6,* 1–10.

Shlien, J. M. (1970). Phenomenology and personality. In J. T. Hart & T. M. Tomlinson (Eds.), *New directions in client-centered therapy* (pp. 95–128). Boston: Houghton-Mifflin.

Smith, T. W., Kendall, P. C., & Keefe, F. J. (Eds.). (2002). Special issue: Behavioral medicine and clinical health psychology. *Journal of Consulting and Clinical Psychology, 70,* 459–856.

Sobel, D. S. (1994). Mind matters, money matters: The cost-effectiveness of clinical behavioral medicine. In S. Blumenthal, K. Matthews, & S. Weiss (Eds.), *New research frontiers in behavioral medicine: Proceedings of the national conference.* Washington, DC: National Institutes of Health.

Sternberg, R. J. (2003). President's column: Unify! *Monitor on Psychology, 34(2),* 5.

Sternberg, R. J. , & Grigorenko, E. L. (2001). Unified psychology. *American Psychologist, 56,* 1069–1079.

U.S. Government Accounting Office. (1999). *Report to the chairman and ranking minority member, Committee on Armed Services, U.S. Senate* (GA)/HEHS-99-98). Washington, DC: Author.

VandenBos, G., DeLeon, P., & Belar, C. (1991). How many psychological practitioners are needed? It's too early to know! *Professional Psychology: Research and Practice, 22,* 441–448.

Vector Research. (1996, May 17). *Cost-effectiveness and feasibility of the DoD psychopharmacology demonstration project: Final Report (ES-5).* Arlington, VA: Author.

8

PARADIGMS, NARRATIVES, AND PLURALISM IN UNDERGRADUATE PSYCHOLOGY

THOMAS V. McGOVERN AND CHARLES L. BREWER

In his history of undergraduate education, Rudolph wrote,

> The curriculum began as an import, arriving in the intellectual baggage of the settlers of Massachusetts Bay. Over three hundred years of change have given it a thoroughly American character, reflecting the diversity and flexibility of the culture around it, lending itself to society's major purposes. . . . Curricular history is American history and therefore carries the burden of revealing the central purposes and driving directions of American society. (1977, pp. 23–24)

More than 200 years after the first curriculum at Harvard College educated 17th-century men preparing for the ministry, Francis Wayland of Brown University observed in 1855 that "the American people expected the colleges to educate a democracy of talents and a democracy of vocations" (as cited in Rudolph, 1977, p. 111). In 1868, Cornell University opened its doors with the motto "any person—any study" (Levine & Nidiffer, 1997, p. 71). Undergraduate education is rooted in this American tradition of diverse institutions offering sundry academic programs. After World War II, curricula were designed for students with even more diverse characteristics (i.e., age, gender, socioeconomic status, and ethnicity), using increasingly varied delivery systems (e.g., compressed semesters, asynchronous distance learning, and so forth) to achieve universal access.

Like academic colleagues in other arts and sciences fields, psychologists often proclaim that a common goal of undergraduate education is "to teach the discipline" and to do so as part of a student's liberal arts education. Ratcliff's analysis of a *discipline* in higher education is helpful to understand the undergraduate curriculum as a potential source of unity, despite different institutional missions and increasingly different populations of students.

> A *discipline* is literally what the term implies. . . . Disciplines can provide a conceptual framework for understanding what knowledge is and how it is acquired. Disciplinary learning provides a logical structure to relationships between concepts, propositions, common paradigms, and organizing principles. Disciplines develop themes, canons, and grand narratives to join different streams of research in the field and to provide meaningful conceptualizations and frameworks for further analysis. . . . Discipline-based curricula are a social construction developed by academics . . . their organization and representation of what is worth knowing and why. (1997, pp. 14–15)

The curricular history of psychology reflects the construction of our scientific discipline in paradigmatic terms. The historian of psychology, Leahey (1992), reminded us that Kuhn's (1962/1970) revised schema for scientific paradigms included a "shared exemplar" (i.e., an ideal model of research) and a "disciplinary matrix" (i.e., the metatheoretical, philosophical, and metaphysical beliefs of a particular scientific community). Perhaps more important for psychologists' commitments to scholarly work and their students' education, "in Kuhn's hands science becomes an intellectual adventure, paradigm making being human creativity at its highest pitch and greatest influence" (Leahey, 1992, p. 310). However, Driver-Linn's (2003) critique of psychologists' use of Kuhn is especially important to keep in mind: "Kuhn chatter in psychology reflects earnestly held concerns about divisions in the field, divisions that have arisen because scientific psychology necessarily encompasses both natural science and social science traditions, which represent competing positions on truth and progress" (p. 269).

As befits the development of a paradigm, reformers of undergraduate disciplinary education have attempted to agree on primary characteristics, but earlier efforts to identify a common curriculum have shifted more recently to defining common learning outcomes. Benjamin's (2001) analysis of psychology's struggles with articulating a core curriculum at any level of education lamented the absence of a common course of study. He examined proponents' arguments that, without it, specialization and fragmentation would remain the order of the day; and he maintained that important scientific advances come from individuals broadly educated by a core curriculum and who can thereby navigate across theoretical and methodological boundaries more easily.

Although the American Psychological Association (APA) endorsed a specific set of National Standards for the Teaching of High School Psychology (Brewer, 1999), it has not done so for undergraduate or graduate education. By the end of the 20th century, the APA had approved a set of *Quality Principles for Undergraduate Psychology Education* (McGovern & Reich, 1996) and its Board of Educational Affairs (BEA) had endorsed a report on undergraduate psychology major learning goals and outcomes (Halonen, 2002).

Advocates for curricular diversity argue that psychology has no "core" because its span of knowledge is so broad and so complex. Educational programs must provide their students a depth in their learning based on specialized faculty expertise and institutional missions. This is the only bulwark against shallow expertise for a scientist or practitioner in training. An alternative response to fragmentation can be found in Sternberg and Grigorenko (2001), who argued that *"unified psychology* is the multiparadigmatic, multidisciplinary, and integrated study of psychological phenomena through converging operations" (p. 1069). Identifying scholars and the knowledge they produce in the traditional categories of psychological subdisciplines with singular methodologies and paradigms are "bad habits" that need to be evaluated and probably modified. The historian, Driver-Linn (2003), felt the same way, urging "a value placed on synthesis, meta-analytic perspective, and cross-area expertise. Why then, in practice, are history of psychology and philosophy of science relatively undervalued and breadth routinely sacrificed in favor of specialization?" (p. 276).

In McGovern and Brewer (2003), we traced the history of undergraduate psychology education using three traditional aspects of faculty life— teaching, scholarship, and service—as an organizing framework. In this chapter, we focus on the undergraduate curriculum and psychologists' efforts to create a disciplinary paradigm. We have been staunch advocates for an undergraduate curriculum that is grounded in a liberal arts tradition, *and* responsive to the vocational aspirations of our students, *and* reflects faculty expertise at particular institutions. However, from our service in local, regional, and national contexts; from having been consultants to many departments; and from our numerous roles in association governance and campus administrations, we are often confronted by the dilemmas inherent in having or not having a unified undergraduate psychology curriculum. Motivated by Sternberg's goal for this book, we want to raise questions about the limitations of pursuing a singular paradigm as scholars and as teachers of the discipline. Perhaps a new century calls for us to embrace multiple paradigms and, as Leahey concluded, "In place of a story of revolutions, one can tell psychology's story as a narrative of research traditions" (1992, p. 316). This is what we will propose as an alternative strategy to tell the story of psychology; it will require a renewed commitment to pluralism and its thorough integration into the undergraduate curriculum.

UNDERGRADUATE PSYCHOLOGY IN THE
CENTURY OF THE MAJOR

In his analysis of the progressive era from 1870 to 1910, Veysey (1973) attributed profound changes to three forces that crystallized for the first time and shaped so many later practices in American higher education: (a) utilitarian needs of American society, (b) advent of science and an increasing respect for empirical evidence in the construction and applications of knowledge, and (c) a reaffirmed belief in the historical tradition of liberal education to promote a responsible citizenry.

Before this era, receiving an *artium baccalaureatum* signified that a student had mastered a unified curriculum with common general education courses and a narrow set of specialized concentrations. The Morrill Land-Grant Act of 1862 increased the number of state universities and fostered a more utilitarian perspective for the curriculum. Professional education in agriculture and engineering spawned many new pathways to an undergraduate degree. Alternatively, the German model for the American research university exemplified the new force of science with its focus on graduate training and increased specialization in undergraduate education. Faculty increased their emphasis on research, founding professional associations through which scholars in the humanities, social sciences, and natural sciences shared their findings and built the theoretical and methodological knowledge bases of new intellectual fields. Established in 1892, the APA was

> one of seven learned societies founded at the turn of the 20th century (Modern Language Association in 1883; American Historical Association in 1884; American Economics Association in 1884; American Philosophical Association in 1901; American Political Science Association in 1904; and American Sociological Society in 1905). (McGovern, 1992, p. 14)

Science and the utilitarian needs of society launched the century of the academic "major." The historical tradition of liberal education gave way to an emphasis on depth rather than breadth as the measure of an educated person.

A 20th-century blueprint for the psychology major could be seen in 1900 at Columbia University in the Department of Philosophy, Psychology, Anthropology, and Education. The introductory course was taught over two semesters, with students studying James's *The Principles of Psychology*, with discussions, practical exercises, and recitation sessions during the first semester. In the second semester, the Introduction to Psychology course covered the "subject matter and methods of modern psychology" (*Columbia University in the City of New York Catalogue*, 1900–1901, p. 176): history of psychology; physiological, experimental, genetic, comparative, pathological, and general psychology; and philosophy of mind. These introductory topics previewed 13 subsequent topic courses, laboratory courses, or supervised research courses.

As more institutions offered psychology courses and programs, the APA sponsored a national study. In its monograph, Sanford (1910) summarized responses from 32 universities with laboratories and indicated that psychologists were already teaching the first course in sections of 200, 300, and 400 students; Whipple (1910) reported a mean enrollment of 107 students for his 100 normal school respondents. In institutions with laboratories, Sanford reported that 25% of the instructors saw the course as a gateway to the study of philosophy; more than 50% wanted students to study science for its own sake as well as to apply psychological principles to life. Calkins's (1910) summary from institutions with no laboratories highlights how important she thought it was for faculty to distinguish psychology's content and methods from its philosophical antecedents and how the introductory course should be embedded within the undergraduate curriculum:

> Psychology is psychology whatever the use to be made of it. *First courses in psychology should therefore be essentially the same in content and in method,* whether they introduce the student to advanced work in psychology or to the different problems of pedagogy, of ethics or of metaphysics. [T]he immediate purpose of every course in psychology is to make the student expert in the study of himself: to lead him to isolate, analyze, to classify, and (in the scientific, not in the metaphysical sense) to explain his own perceiving, remembering, thinking, feeling, and willing. (emphasis in original; 1910, p. 45)

Summarizing these reports from different types of institutions, Seashore (1910) proposed three common curricular goals: (a) teach psychology as a science with incidental treatment of its application, (b) train students in observation and explanation of mental facts, and (c) offer a balanced survey of all topics that psychologists study with an in-depth examination of a few.

Wolfle reviewed the literature published on the introductory course since the 1910 studies and distilled the goals espoused for the first course into four objectives: (a) teach facts and principles, (b) develop scientific method or habits of critical thought, (c) prepare students for later courses or interest in psychology, and (d) eliminate popular superstition. Evaluating more than 100 studies from the first 50 years of psychology's history, he concluded that "we are still debating many of the same issues and being embarrassed by the same difficulties. Many of the same recommendations considered necessary in 1909 are still necessary in 1942" (Wolfle, 1942, p. 686).

THE PSYCHOLOGY MAJOR FROM 1950 TO 2000

Scholars from the Carnegie Foundation for the Advancement of Teaching (1977) described the period of curricular expansion after World War II as "the academic shopping center" (p. 5). Rapidly increasing enrollments and course proliferation characterized the period from 1950 to 1975. Sanford and Fleishman (1950) found 261 different course titles in their study of a random sample of 330 institutional catalogs. Lux and Daniel found 1,356 different titles, "a 'course title inflation' of 519%, or about 19% per year on the average, from 1947 to 1975" (1978, p. 13).

As these centrifugal forces grew more powerful, however, conservative and centripetal functions of the learned societies came into play. The APA, with funding support from other sponsors, exerted its unifying influence by holding a series of national conferences and meetings on the undergraduate curriculum from 1950 to the end of the 20th century. Lloyd and Brewer (1992) reviewed reports from the Cornell Conference (Buxton et al., 1952); Michigan Conference (McKeachie & Milholland, 1961); Kulik (1973); APA/Association of American Colleges Project on Liberal Learning, Study-in-Depth, and the Arts and Sciences Major—Psychology (McGovern, Furumoto, Halpern, Kimble, & McKeachie, 1991); and the St. Mary's College of Maryland Conference held in 1991 (McGovern, 1993). Authors of the conference reports tried to discern unifying themes for undergraduate psychology amid constant expansion of psychological knowledge and methodologies as well as considerable variability in curricula to cover the discipline's increasing complexity.

Buxton et al. identified four objectives of undergraduate psychology:

1. intellectual development and a liberal education;
2. a knowledge of psychology, its research findings, its major problems, its theoretical integrations, and its contributions;
3. personal growth and an increased ability to meet personal and social adjustment problems adequately;
4. desirable attitudes and habits of thought, such as the stimulation of intellectual curiosity, respect for others, and a feeling of social responsibility. (1952, pp. 2–3)

The authors proposed one curriculum model. The introductory course was to be followed by five intermediate or core courses (statistics, motivation, perception, thinking and language, and ability), then advanced courses in specialized areas (e.g., social, learning, comparative, physiological, personnel, etc.), and capstone courses in personality and in history and systems. All courses should be taught as "experimental psychology" courses. The authors wrote separate chapters on personal adjustment courses, technical training, implementation problems based on institutional differences, and the need for research to assess the effectiveness of undergraduate education.

McKeachie and Milholland (1961) used survey data from 411 responding departments; 274 reported revising their curricula since the Cornell report. Demographics of higher education had changed, in terms of increased numbers of students representing greater diversity in age and vocational goals, but McKeachie and Milholland suggested that "more serious than the problem of sheer numbers is the fact that teaching is not a prestigeful occupation in psychology these days. The research man is the status figure" (1961, p. 6). The authors urged that the psychology curriculum "be firmly anchored in the liberal arts, rejecting undergraduate vocational training as a primary goal" (p. 33). The greatest value was in "teaching psychology as an organized body of scientific knowledge and method with its own internal structure for determining the admissibility of materials to be taught" (p. 59). They were unequivocal in their commitment to teaching psychology as a continually advancing science, reaffirming the Cornell group's objectives: content knowledge, rigorous habits of thought, and values and attitudes. This report contained three curricular models because the Michigan Conference faculty could not agree on a single one.

Capturing the profound changes in demographics and curricula on college campuses during the 1960s, Kulik's national survey and case studies of undergraduate departments and their highly diverse curricula led him to conclude the following:

> It is an empirical question whether curricula like those of liberal arts colleges best meet the ideals of liberal education. Is it conceivable that for some students, occupationally oriented programs may provide a better road to personal soundness than the traditional curricula of liberal arts colleges? (1973, p. 202)

Kulik's insightful conclusion was influential during the 1980s and 1990s: "The diverse goals of students in psychology courses suggest that pluralism may be a valuable concept in the design of programs in psychology" (Kulik, 1973, p. 203). This comment reflected the empirical realities of what Kulik found in undergraduate psychology. To us, it frames the dilemma of pursuing a single paradigm for undergraduate psychology, and we say more about pluralism later in this chapter.

Responding to different institutional missions, different faculty, different students, and different programs created problems for all higher education in the 1980s. Blue-ribbon panels decried the loss of common purpose and coherence in undergraduate programs. Off-campus critics diagnosed the problem with undergraduate education as an overemphasis on faculty research and the related priority given to graduate education, especially at research universities where undergraduates were herded into large auditoriums and often taught by inexperienced instructors. On-campus reformers advocated greater balance between a common, unifying liberal arts education and the demands for specialized major fields of study. Almost everyone agreed that it was time to clarify the goals and methods of undergraduate education in specific departments and across the campus. A renewed emphasis on liberal arts education became a nostalgic mantra, but it was a major catalyst for curricular evaluation.

In 1983, the APA Council of Representatives reaffirmed that the psychology baccalaureate is a liberal arts degree, that no prescribed curriculum should be developed but that guidelines or models could be considered based on continuing, periodic surveys of undergraduate education. At the 1991 St. Mary's Conference, 60 faculty members from research and comprehensive universities, liberal arts and community colleges, and high schools met to articulate common understandings for undergraduate psychology. Their collective efforts yielded the *Handbook for Enhancing Undergraduate Education in Psychology* (McGovern, 1993) and the *Quality Principles for Undergraduate Psychology Education* (McGovern & Reich, 1996).

At St. Mary's, Brewer et al.'s curriculum team reaffirmed the study of psychology as a liberal arts discipline, asserting that "the fundamental goal of education in psychology, from which all the others follow, is to teach students to think as scientists about behavior" (1993, p. 168). They amplified this statement with six specific goals: (a) attention to human diversity, (b) breadth and depth of knowledge, (c) methodological competence, (d) practical experience and applications, (e) communication skills, and (f) sensitivity to ethical issues. These authors recommended a sequence of courses to accomplish these goals: introductory course, methodology courses, content courses, and an integrative or capstone experience. Content courses should be balanced between the natural science and social science knowledge bases of an increasingly complex discipline.

When Perlman and McCann (1999b) reviewed structures of undergraduate curricula in 500 catalogs, they found that the St. Mary's Conference, like its predecessors, had intended consequences as well as areas of minimal influence. Although a senior capstone experience was advocated by every group since the Cornell Conference, this recommendation remained unheeded, particularly in doctoral institutions. The same was true for the teaching of psychometric methods as part of a core methodology trio of courses with statistics and experimental psychology. Fiscal, staffing, and space problems were cited as primary obstacles to the development and maintenance of laboratory facilities. Their conclusions about the undergraduate psychology curriculum at the end of the 20th century follow.

The Cornell report's (Buxton et al., 1952) emphasis on teaching psychology as a scientific discipline in the liberal arts tradition remains current.

The required core as recommended by the St. Mary's report (Brewer et al., 1993) as implemented by departments seems to cover "both natural science and social science aspects of psychology" (1952, pp. 175–176).

THE ASSESSMENT MOVEMENT IN HIGHER EDUCATION AND IN PSYCHOLOGY

Continuing discontent with undergraduate education prompted a new movement—assessing student learning outcomes. A report by the Study Group on the Conditions of Excellence in American Higher Education (1984) was aptly titled *Involvement in Learning*. The authors identified three key factors to change business as usual: (a) set clear and high expectations for learning, (b) engage students more actively in learning, and (c) provide direct feedback and systematic assessment of students' progress. Ewell (2002) ascribed the movement's birth to the first national conference on assessment sponsored by the Association of American Higher Education in 1985. The Association of American Colleges' (AAC) multidisciplinary effort, Project on Liberal Learning, Study-in-Depth, and the Arts and Sciences Major (1991a, 1991b) synthesized demands for a renewed emphasis on high expectations, curricular coherence, and the assessment of student learning outcomes.

In paradigmatic terms, the focus of reform shifted from measuring inputs (e.g., curriculum and student–faculty ratios) as correlates of quality to assessing outputs directly (e.g., students' knowledge of major fields). In narrative terms, the metaphors used on and off campus shifted from improving the quality of teaching to measuring the quantity and environmental qualities of student learning. The APA sponsored one of the disciplinary teams for the AAC project, and their final report (McGovern et al., 1991) influenced participants' discussions at the St. Mary's Conference. The undergraduate psychology story shifted to the assessment of student learning outcomes during the 1990s. Halpern (1988) predicted as much; Halpern (2004) and Pusateri (2002) documented the rationale, methods, and accomplishments of the discipline's responses to this potent new movement.

PARADIGMATIC OUTCOMES AT THE END OF THE 20TH CENTURY

McGovern et al. (1991) identified eight common goals for the diversity of settings, students, and courses that characterized psychology: (a) knowledge base, (b) thinking skills, (c) language skills, (d) information gathering and synthesis skills, (e) research methods and statistical skills,

(f) interpersonal skills, (g) history of psychology, and (h) ethics and values. At St. Mary's, Halpern et al. (1993) mapped a comprehensive outcomes assessment program for psychology. Their list of desired outcomes for undergraduate psychology included knowledge base (e.g., content areas, methods, theory, and history); intellectual skills (e.g., thinking, communication, information gathering, and synthesis skills, and quantitative, scientific, and technological skills); and personal characteristics (e.g., interpersonal and intrapersonal skills, motivation, ethics, and sensitivity to people and cultures). The authors advocated a multimethod, matrix approach, including archival forms of assessment data, classroom assessment, standardized testing, course-embedded assessment, portfolio analysis, interviews, external examiners, performance-based assessment strategies, and assessment of critical thinking.

Through the APA-sponsored Psychology Partnerships Project held in 1999, faculty continued the work on assessment of student learning outcomes. The BEA approved the Undergraduate Psychology Major Learning Goals and Outcomes (Halonen, 2002). This document listed 48 student learning outcomes, with several discrete elements for 10 common learning goals to be expected across educational contexts. The goals were organized in two categories: knowledge, skills, and values consistent with the science and application of psychology (goals 1 through 5) and knowledge, skills, and values, consistent with liberal arts education that are further developed in psychology (goals 6 through 10): This document specified that students should

1. demonstrate familiarity with the major concepts, theoretical perspectives, empirical findings, and historical trends in psychology;
2. understand and apply basic research methods in psychology, including research design, data analysis, and interpretation;
3. respect and use critical and creative thinking, skeptical inquiry, and, when possible, the scientific approach to solve problems related to behavior and mental processes;
4. understand and apply psychological principles to personal, social, and organizational issues;
5. weigh evidence, tolerate ambiguity, act ethically, and reflect other values that are the underpinnings of psychology as a discipline;
6. demonstrate information competencies and the ability to use computers and other technology for many purposes;
7. communicate effectively in a variety of formats;
8. recognize, understand, and respect the complexity of sociocultural and international diversity;

9. develop insight into their own and others' behavior and mental processes and apply effective strategies for self-management and self-improvement; and

10. emerge from the major with realistic ideas about how to implement their psychological knowledge, skills, and values in occupational pursuits in a variety of settings. (Halonen, 2002, pp. 8–9)

Halonen et al. (2003) continued their work from the Psychology Partnerships Project to produce "a rubric for learning, teaching, and assessing scientific inquiry in psychology" (p. 196). They identified eight critical dimensions as one axis of a matrix: (a) descriptive skills, (b) conceptualization skills, (c) problem-solving skills, (d) ethical reasoning, (e) scientific values and attitudes, (f) communication skills, (g) collaboration skills, and (h) self-assessment. As the second axis, the authors proposed five developmental levels of increasing proficiency as students progress through any psychology curriculum: (a) before training; (b) introductory psychology; (c) developing level after several required or elective courses; (d) integrating level at the capstone course stage; and (e) a professional level of proficiency expected on completion of graduate training and entry into early career settings.

The book *Measuring Up: Educational Assessment Challenges and Practices for Psychology* (Dunn, Mehrotra, & Halonen, 2004) should become a touchstone text in this movement. Chapter authors provided a cornucopia of scholarly, rigorous, empirically based case studies about assessing student learning outcomes in psychology. In the 15 years after Halpern's (1988) influential article, assessment became part of the culture of undergraduate education, with increasingly reflective practitioners in the discipline of psychology. The shift from teaching to learning is now embedded in the literature.

Does this state of affairs suggest that paradigmatic unity has been achieved?

DISCIPLINARY PARADIGMS AND PLURALISTIC NARRATIVES

Benjamin's (2001) concluding reflections suggest what needs to come next (for graduate and undergraduate education) in a discipline-based paradigm.

Historically, psychologists have never been either able or willing to answer the question, "What is a psychologist?" Scientists are trained to be independent, to be skeptical, and to recognize the transient nature of truths. Furthermore, scientists are trained to ask questions about cause and effect. With respect to a core curriculum, they want assurance of a demonstrated relationship between required courses and scientific and professional competencies. It is not obvious that such relationships have been demonstrated. (2001, p. 741)

What has not been demonstrated?

First, for 100 years, but especially in the past 20 years, psychologists crafted increasingly specific and directly measurable learning outcomes for undergraduates. Educators in the discipline also have a sophisticated portfolio of best assessment practices (Dunn et al., 2004). Our careful reading of conference reports; case study literature; and the APA-endorsed statements of principles, goals, and outcomes suggests that there is now a high level of consistency in what experts espouse as the outcomes of undergraduate psychology programs.

Second, for almost 50 years, psychologists sought the holy grail of a common curriculum. Perlman and McCann concluded,

> Many frequently offered courses have been found for decades and 13 such courses first listed by Henry (1938) are in the present Top 30. Some courses are slowly being replaced. Thus, the curriculum reflects both continuity and slow change, perhaps due to the time that it takes for theory, research, and discourse to define new subdiscipline areas or perhaps due to department inertia and resistance to modifying the curriculum. (1999a, p. 181)

Our experiences as program consultants have convinced us that there will always be variability in undergraduate curricula, reflecting differences in institutions' missions and faculty expertise. Nevertheless, we also believe that curricular similarities are now more prevalent than differences.

Third, we are still at an early stage in demonstrating what types of students seek what types of outcomes and thereby benefit most from what types of courses and teaching strategies. McGovern et al. noted in their APA/AAC project report:

> Comments on an earlier draft of this article also pointed to different views on how best to integrate gender, ethnicity, culture, and class into the study of psychology. . . . Most psychologists would acknowledge that faculty members must challenge campus racism and sexism, but there is less agreement on how to do so. Gender, ethnicity, culture, and class are seen by some teachers as issues that challenge the contemporary curricula. Such a challenge also questions traditional research methodologies that are empirical, quantitative, and positivist, and may advocate alternative psychological methods that are contextual, interpretive, and more qualitative. Other psychologists believe that, although these topics and the new knowledge generated by research have legitimacy in the discipline, they should be subtopics best left to treatments determined by an instructor's sensitivities and commitments. (1991, pp. 599–600)

Driver-Linn (2003) examined how the "science wars" continue and are at the root of the perceptions of psychology as horribly fractionated, of being immersed in a perpetual identity crisis. The dispute about what constitutes "good science" remains paramount. Are scientific laws and truth obtained from rigorous methods that "winnow away the subjective from the objective" or must we acknowledge that the "objective cannot be winnowed from the subjective"? (p. 270).

The St. Mary's Conference participants represented commendable diversity on gender, ethnicity, and educational settings; a chapter on celebrating a "psychology of variance" (Puente et al., 1993) was one tangible result. Recent efforts to stimulate discussions about diversification in psychology are instructive (e.g., Balls Organista, Chun, & Marin, 2000; Gloria, Rieckmann, & Rush, 2000; Hill, 2000; Kowalski, 2000; Ocampo et al., 2003; Simoni, Sexton-Radek, Yescavage, Richard, & Lundquist, 1999; Sue, 1999; Sue, Bingham, Porche-Burke, & Vasquez, 1999). Much more work is required, however, to integrate many voices into psychology's story and then to measure directly the differential effects of their variance.

Ash (1983) and Ratcliff (1997) described disciplines as social constructions created by academics and embedded in sociocultural contexts. While affirming the strides made in defining and measuring student learning outcomes, McGovern proposed that continuing to develop a singular paradigm for the discipline will not be enough. "Alas, the rainbow demographics of American society, its complex problems, and the interconnectivity that persons create and technology enables all suggest the need for a 21st-century, postdisciplinary liberal arts in higher education" (2004, 270). In the 21st century, we are now witnessing a redefinition of discipline-based undergraduate education as part of academic and societal movements already under way.

The Association of American Colleges and Universities, via its American Commitments Project (National Panel on American Commitments: Diversity, Democracy, and Liberal Learning, 1995) raised serious questions about the effectiveness of our efforts to teach students about democratic community building and pluralistic thinking. Based on their review of cross-disciplinary higher education literature, Schneider and Schoenberg (1998) identified five emerging goals of liberal learning: (a) acquiring intellectual skills or capacities; (b) understanding multiple modes of inquiry and approaches to knowledge; (c) developing societal, civic, and global knowledge; (d) gaining self-knowledge and grounded values; and (e) working on a concentration and integration of learning. These are not philosophical statements about general education; they are student learning outcomes for broad liberal arts courses taken by all students and for courses in various academic majors.

What should be psychology's response to these changing definitions of the liberal arts? We echo the tradition in the curricular reports and the statements about student outcomes issued since 1990 that learning the history of psychology must be demonstrated in all curricula. More than any other material, readings in history provide all students, but especially psychology majors, with an understanding of paradigms and pluralism, of the sociocultural bases for basic and applied research perspectives, and the origins of the different ways of doing science espoused by their different faculty who still live under the same roof. Menu-plan curriculum requirements are not just political treaties to achieve a modicum of civility at departmental faculty meetings; as we noted in our introduction by Driver-Linn's (2003) commentary on Kuhnian devotion, they reflect deeply inherent conflicts between social science and natural science perspectives.

On just this issue, a historical perspective could enhance students' liberal learning. For example, Cahan and White (1992) reviewed "proposals for a second psychology," excavating its roots in Wundt's *Volkerpsychologie*; in James's, Baldwin's, Mead's, and Dewey's emphases on the social and political intersections with psychology; and in Vygotsky's appreciation for the multiplicities of psychology. Cahan and White concluded that psychology "fell into two scientific families: one a natural–scientific explanatory psychology and the other a descriptive, philosophical–phenomenological psychology" (p. 230). They also described how such divergent views were received in the first half of the 20th century by the experimentalists invested in building a singular paradigm. "As psychology grew larger, the pluralism of members' interests hardened into the politics of the subdisciplines. . . . Psychology has always been multiparadigmatic and there are probably fundamental reasons why it ought to be so . . . One of the critical problems for psychology, in every period of its existence, has been the management of this basic and useful pluralism" (p. 229). Without a sense of psychology's intellectual history, without faculty unpackaging their assumptions about Kuhn's "shared exemplar" and "disciplinary matrix," students will understand differences of ideas as either/or propositions. Whether students' understanding of the origins and evolution of diverse ideas generalizes to greater tolerance for pluralism in their civic communities is an empirical question. We believe, however, that any hope for unity must be grounded in this cognitive understanding and its affective and behavioral consequences. Undergraduate psychology education is one of the best and most popular contemporary sites for such learning to take place.

CONCLUSION

We began this chapter with the premise that curricular history is American history. While we were writing this chapter, four news stories illustrated the importance of pursuing unifying principles and strategies for undergraduate psychology education in the 21st century. First, one state's board of regents raised admissions standards for new first-year students at all state-funded universities. This change followed approval of the largest tuition increase in history. Public statements by university presidents contained a plethora of supporting data about "doing no harm" to those most in need of higher education or to those least able to afford it. Second, after being excluded from a graduation party at a private residence, a 16-year-old student returned to the scene with a gun, shot into the crowd, and killed an honors student. Shocked parents and students wondered why this horrendous act occurred. Third, the nation now realizes that the ousted regime in Iraq may be replaced by leaders who are different from those the administration hoped to install. American pluralism and democratic decision making may not be easily transportable to cultures with histories, economies, religions, and geopolitics that are different from ours. Fourth, President George W. Bush announced the reappointment of Alan Greenspan as Chair of the Federal Reserve System. One high-level official opined that this was an excellent decision because our economy is now based more on psychological factors than on economic ones. Does the public's faith rest on a cult of personality—with psychology as its basis—that trumps data-based decision making, with economics as its exemplar? What does such thinking say about the public's understanding of scientific psychology and its core values?

How did the study of psychology help graduates in the Class of 2003 understand these issues? Using statistical information to influence attitudes about educational access and excellence, the complex origins and prevalence of violence in our society, ethnic and cultural differences, distinguishing between correlation and causation—will our undergraduate psychology students make appropriate connections between what they learned in their classes and these real-world problems?

Should we pose similar questions to faculty colleagues in other disciplines of the arts and sciences? Should we reconsider the historical boundaries between liberal arts education and disciplinary specialization in academic majors? Should we forego traditional paradigmatic approaches to unity and build interdisciplinary curricula, grounded in a historical perspective, for 21st-century problems and for our students who will be asked to solve them? The themes, canons, and grand narratives of our socially constructed academic discipline have been composed so that psychological language and assumptions permeate almost every facet of contemporary American society. Sternberg and Grigorenko's (2001) appeal for "a vintage old wine in a new and better bottle" (p. 1078) is a provocative stimulus to begin discussing a new story.

As idealistic optimists, we are reassured by the continuing popularity of undergraduate psychology. As realistic skeptics, we are challenged to build on this success in ways that may lead us into less familiar territories, to meet colleagues in the liberal arts with different assumptions, and to construct courses and programs with fuzzier boundaries. This fascinating new story will be captured in a narrative with a theme of pluridisciplinarity. Experience has taught us that less unity can be more fun!

REFERENCES

Ash, M. G. (1983). The self-presentation of a discipline: History of psychology in the United States between pedagogy and scholarship. In L. Graham, W. Lepenies, & P. Weingart (Eds.), *Functions and uses of disciplinary histories* (pp. 143–189). Boston: D. Reidel.

Balls Organista, P., Chun, K. M., & Marin, G. (2000). Teaching an undergraduate course on ethnic diversity. *Teaching of Psychology, 27,* 12–17.

Benjamin, L. T., Jr. (2001). American psychology's struggles with its curriculum: Should a thousand flowers bloom? *American Psychologist, 56,* 735–742.

Brewer, C. L. (Ed.). (1999). *National standards for the teaching of high school psychology.* Washington, DC: American Psychological Association.

Brewer, C. L., Hopkins, J. R., Kimble, G. A., Matlin, M. W., McCann, L. I., McNeil, O. V., et al. (1993). Curriculum. In T. V. McGovern (Ed.), *Handbook for enhancing undergraduate education in psychology* (pp. 161–182). Washington, DC: American Psychological Association.

Buxton, C. E., Cofer, C. N., Gustad, J. W., MacLeod, R. B., McKeachie, W. J., & Wolfle, D. (1952). *Improving undergraduate instruction in psychology.* New York: Macmillan.

Cahan, E. D., & White, S. H. (1992). Proposals for a second psychology. *American Psychologist, 47,* 224–235.

Calkins, M. W. (1910). The teaching of elementary psychology in colleges supposed to have no laboratory. *Psychological Monographs, 12*(4, Whole No. 51), 41–53.

Carnegie Foundation for the Advancement of Teaching. (1977). *Missions of the college curriculum: A contemporary review with suggestions.* San Francisco: Jossey-Bass.

Columbia University in the City of New York Catalogue. (1900–1901). New York: Columbia University.

Driver-Linn, E. (2003). Where is psychology going? Structural fault lines revealed by psychologists' use of Kuhn. *American Psychologist, 58,* 269–278.

Dunn, D. S., Mehrotra, C. M., & Halonen, J. S. (Eds.). (2004). *Measuring up: Educational assessment challenges and practices for psychology.* Washington, DC: American Psychological Association.

Ewell, P. T. (2002). An emerging scholarship: A brief history of assessment. In T. W. Banta & Associates (Eds.), *Building a scholarship of assessment* (pp. 3–25). San Francisco: Jossey-Bass.

Gloria, A. M., Rieckmann, T. T., & Rush, J. D. (2000). Issues and recommendations for teaching an ethnic/culture-based course. *Teaching of Psychology, 27*, 102–107.

Halonen, J. S. (Ed.). (2002). *Undergraduate psychology major learning goals and outcomes: A report.* Retrieved May 2, 2004, from http://www.apa.org/ed/pcue/taskforcereport2.pdf

Halonen, J. S., Bosack, T., Clay, S, McCarthy, M., Dunn, D. S., Hill, G. W., IV, et al. (2003). A rubric for learning, teaching, and assessing scientific inquiry in psychology. *Teaching of Psychology, 30*, 196–208.

Halpern, D. F. (1988). Assessing student outcomes for psychology majors. *Teaching of Psychology, 15*, 181–186.

Halpern, D. F. (2004). Outcomes assessment 101. In D. S. Dunn, C. M. Mehrotra, & J. S. Halonen (Eds.), *Measuring up: Educational assessment challenges and practices for psychology.* Washington, DC: American Psychological Association.

Halpern, D. F., Appleby, D. C., Beers, S. E., Cowan, C. L., Furedy, J. J., Halonen, J. S., et al. (1993). Targeting outcomes: Covering your assessment concerns and needs. In T. V. McGovern (Ed.), *Handbook for enhancing undergraduate education in psychology* (pp. 23–46). Washington, DC: American Psychological Association.

Henry, E. R. (1938). A survey of courses in psychology offered by undergraduate colleges of liberal arts. *Psychological Bulletin, 35*, 430–435.

Hill, G. W., IV. (2000). Incorporating a cross-cultural perspective in the undergraduate psychology curriculum: An interview with David Matsumoto. *Teaching of Psychology, 27*, 71–75.

Kowalski, R. M. (2000). Including gender, race, and ethnicity in psychology content courses. *Teaching of Psychology, 27*, 18–24.

Kuhn, T. S. (1970). *The structure of scientific revolutions* (Rev. ed.). Chicago: University of Chicago Press. (Original work published 1962)

Kulik, J. (1973). *Undergraduate education in psychology.* Washington, DC: American Psychological Association.

Leahey, T. H. (1992). The mythical revolutions of American psychology. *American Psychologist, 47*, 308–318.

Levine, A., & Nidiffer, J. (1997). Key turning points in the evolving curriculum. In J. G. Gaff, J. L. Ratcliff, & Associates (Eds.), *Handbook of the undergraduate curriculum: A comprehensive guide to purposes, structures, practices, and change* (pp. 53–85). San Francisco: Jossey-Bass.

Lloyd, M. A., & Brewer, C. L. (1992). National conferences on undergraduate psychology. In A. E. Puente, J. R. Matthews, & C. L. Brewer (Eds.), *Teaching psychology in America: A history* (pp. 263–284). Washington, DC: American Psychological Association.

Lux, D. F., & Daniel, R. S. (1978). Which courses are most frequently listed by psychology departments? *Teaching of Psychology, 5*, 13–16.

McGovern, T. V. (1992). Evolution of undergraduate curricula in psychology, 1892–1992. In A. E. Puente, J. R. Matthews, & C. L. Brewer (Eds.), *Teaching psychology in America: A history* (pp. 13–38). Washington, DC: American Psychological Association.

McGovern, T. V. (Ed.). (1993). *Handbook for enhancing undergraduate education in psychology*. Washington, DC: American Psychological Association.

McGovern, T. V. (2004). Liberal arts, diverse lives, and assessing psychology. In D. S. Dunn, C. M. Mehrotra, & J. S. Halonen (Eds.), *Measuring up: Educational assessment challenges and practices for psychology*. Washington, DC: American Psychological Association.

McGovern, T. V., & Brewer, C. L. (2003). Undergraduate education. In D. K. Freedheim (Ed.), *History of psychology* (Vol. I, pp. 465–481). New York: Wiley.

McGovern, T. V., Furumoto, L., Halpern, D. F., Kimble, G. A., & McKeachie, W. J. (1991). Liberal education, study in depth, and the arts and sciences major—Psychology. *American Psychologist, 46*, 598–605.

McGovern, T. V., & Reich, J. N. (1996). A comment on the *Quality Principles. American Psychologist, 51*, 252–255.

McKeachie, W. J., & Milholland, J. E. (1961). *Undergraduate curricula in psychology*. Glenview, IL: Scott, Foresman.

National Panel on American Commitments: Diversity, Democracy, and Liberal Learning. (1995). *The drama of diversity and democracy: Higher education and American commitments*. Washington, DC: Association of American Colleges and Universities.

Ocampo, C., Prieto, L. R., Whittlesey, V., Connor, J., Janco-Gidley, J., Mannix, S., et al. (2003). Diversity research in teaching of psychology: Summary and recommendations. *Teaching of Psychology, 30*, 5–18.

Perlman, B., & McCann, L. I. (1999a). The most frequently listed courses in the undergraduate psychology curriculum. *Teaching of Psychology, 26*, 177–182.

Perlman, B., & McCann, L. I. (1999b). The structure of the psychology undergraduate curriculum. *Teaching of Psychology, 26*, 171–176.

Project on Liberal Learning, Study-in-Depth, and the Arts and Sciences Major. (1991a). *The challenge of connecting learning* (Vol. 1). Washington, DC: Association of American Colleges.

Project on Liberal Learning, Study-in-Depth, and the Arts and Sciences Major. (1991b). *Reports from the fields* (Vol. 2). Washington, DC: Association of American Colleges.

Puente, A. E., Blanch, E., Candland, D. K., Denmark, F. L., Laman, C., Lutsky, N., et al. (1993). Toward a psychology of variance: Increasing the presence and understanding of ethnic minorities in psychology. In T. V. McGovern (Ed.), *Handbook for enhancing undergraduate education in psychology* (pp. 71–92). Washington, DC: American Psychological Association.

Pusateri, T. P. (2002). A decade of changes since the St. Mary's Conference: An interview with Thomas V. McGovern. *Teaching of Psychology, 29*, 76–82.

Ratcliff, J. L. (1997). What is a curriculum and what should it be? In J. G. Gaff, J. L. Ratcliff, & Associates (Eds.), *Handbook of the undergraduate curriculum: A comprehensive guide to purposes, structures, practices, and change* (pp. 5–29). San Francisco: Jossey-Bass.

Rudolph, F. (1977). *Curriculum: A history of the American undergraduate course of study since 1636.* San Francisco: Jossey-Bass.

Sanford, E. C. (1910). The teaching of elementary psychology in colleges and universities with laboratories. *Psychological Monographs, 12*(4, Whole No. 51), 54–71.

Sanford, F. H., & Fleishman, E. A. (1950). A survey of undergraduate psychology courses in American colleges and universities. *American Psychologist, 5,* 33–37.

Schneider, C. G., & Shoenberg, R. (1998). *Contemporary understandings of liberal education.* Washington, DC: Association of American Colleges and Universities.

Seashore, C. E. (1910). General report on the teaching of the elementary course in psychology: Recommendations. *Psychological Monographs, 12*(4, Whole No. 51), 80–91.

Simoni, J. M., Sexton-Radek, K., Yescavage, K., Richard, H., & Lundquist, A. (1999). Teaching diversity: Experiences and recommendations of American Psychological Association Division 2 members. *Teaching of Psychology, 26,* 89–95.

Sternberg, R. J., & Grigorenko, E. L. (2001). Unified psychology. *American Psychologist, 56,* 1069–1079.

Study Group on the Conditions of Excellence in American Higher Education. (1984). *Involvement in learning: Realizing the potential of American higher education.* Washington, DC: U.S. Department of Education.

Sue, D. W., Bingham, R. P., Porche-Burke, L., & Vasquez, M. (1999). The diversification of psychology: A multicultural revolution. *American Psychologist, 54,* 1061–1069.

Sue, S. (1999). Science, ethnicity, and bias: Where have we gone wrong? *American Psychologist, 54,* 1070–1077.

Veysey, L. (1973). Stability and experiment in the American undergraduate curriculum. In C. Kaysen (Ed.), *Content and context: Essays on college education* (pp. 1–63). New York: McGraw-Hill.

Whipple, G. M. (1910). The teaching of psychology in normal schools. *Psychological Monographs, 12*(4, Whole No. 51), 2–40.

Wolfle, D. (1942). The first course in psychology. *Psychological Bulletin, 39,* 685–712.

9

UNIFICATION IN THEORY AND METHOD: POSSIBILITIES AND IMPOSSIBILITIES

JOSEPH F. RYCHLAK

It is ironic that we psychologists are concerned with the unification of our discipline during an age in which diversity is being promoted in the U.S. culture at large. Yancher and Slife (2000, p. 237) have added to the irony by observing that even those psychologists who seek unity lack a uniform decision about how this unity will be achieved. One gets the impression that there is something basically "diverse" about human reasoning. Complexities arise in the meanings advanced. One person has "this" point to make and the other has "that" point to make, and frequently they are saying roughly the same thing from diverse perspectives. In taking up this question of unification I begin with the recognition that my views rest on a few basic assumptions that can help sort out vital aspects of unification. I do not expect to solve the problems inherent to these vital aspects. But I do hope to lend some understanding to what is involved, and based on such knowledge render certain evaluations and predictions concerning both diversity and unification.

THEORY AND METHOD AS DIFFERENT ASPECTS OF
PSYCHOLOGICAL WORK

Although one could begin with any of a number of framing meanings to which unity and diversity would be related, I have settled on two concepts that I believe have great—maybe the greatest—significance for the question of unification in psychology. I refer to the concepts of *theory* and *method*. Here are my definitions of these concepts:

- *Theory*: A series of two or more schematic labels (words, visual images, etc.) that have been hypothesized, presumed, or even factually demonstrated to bear a meaningful relationship, one with the other(s). Theories flow from precedent meanings to consequent meanings, as in: "If it has feathers, webbed feet, a beak, and quacks like a duck, *it's a duck!*" This would be an empirically oriented theory, assigning concept labels to what is literally seen under the *realistic* assumption that perceived reality cannot lie. There are other theorists who believe that reality can indeed lie and that, in fact, it is always created or construed by a person's idealistic biasing thought processes. If we stop to analyze such realistic or *idealistic* processing, it is inevitable that we will find theorizing to be identical to thinking and vice versa!

- *Method*: The means or manner of determining whether a theoretical statement or concept (construct, model, etc.) can be accepted as defensibly true or false. There are basically just two forms of method used in all thought processing, including scientific and mathematical formulations. There is the cognitive (conceptual, etc.) method, which makes use of *procedural evidence,* and the research (measurement, etc.) method, which makes use of *validating evidence* in addition to procedural evidence. Procedural evidence is the sort of proof that enables us to "proceed," to get underway in our thought processing or theorizing. These are the sort of plausibilities that we always affirm as background assumptions based on what we like to call "common sense." Thus, it is common sense that if I want to learn about something like sailing a boat I will have to actually spend time in such a craft, taking instruction from a skilled expert. I begin a search for such an instructor, and when one is located, arrange a time for my lessons. This practical sequence of events is "driven" by the logic of procedural evidence. But now, let us say that I want to pick out a craft for purchase. It would behoove me to seek evidence from actual empirical studies concerning which of those sailboats available has the best track record in performance, including everything from a safety record to the ease with which it can be handled when underway. This empirical interest concerning the actual performance of a craft takes us beyond procedural to validating (i. e., powerfully conclusive) evidence. We are seeking the valid facts, which cannot be solely reasoned but must be reliably observed to exist as predicted by the theoretician. In procedural evidence we dialogue, rely on logic, and try to convince others. In validation we "put up or shut up!"

As psychologists, when we design an experiment according to the rules of science, we are engaging in both theory and method—which is to say that we are going beyond exclusive reliance on procedural plausibilities in hopes of validating our theory based on what it says (i.e., "predicts") will happen empirically. If what our theory predicts actually happens in the experiment designed to test it, we take a certain assurance regarding the validity of our theory. But no theoretical explanation can ever claim certainty. It will always be possible, in principle, to have an alternative explanation of any pattern of empirical facts (Rychlak, 1980). Famous scientists have freely admitted that their theoretical views can and do come into conflict with a colleague's views, and that the only grounds for taking one or the other viewpoint is that of aesthetic preference (Palter, 1956). There is a recognition that theoretical explanations rest on certain assumptions and that it is possible for two different theoreticians to begin their line of thought from contrasting assumptions. I consider this a reflection of the natural process known as *predication* in human reasoning. We humans reason from broad realms of meaning to target some implication, deduction, solution, or conclusion having more specific meanings. The person conceptualizing a "duck" (see earlier discussion) began from a series of meanings having broad reference (i.e., many different birds have feathers, a beak, etc.), but in putting these characteristics together a "singling out" occurred so that a specific referent could be named.

EARLY UNIFICATION AS A RESULT OF
SCHOOLS OF THOUGHT

I believe that diversifying of psychology occurs in two ways: via theory and/or method. When relatively "modern" psychology was introduced in the closing decades of the 19th century there was little to diversify over. The range of application in psychology was relatively narrow. The discipline was struggling to get a foot in the door of academia by endorsing the scientific method of proof—a move that would give it scholarly credentials and thereby the recognition it sought as an academic discipline. Graduate students of that era readily accepted their field as just one more among all other "natural" sciences then in existence. The theoretical language used in this effort was borrowed from these sister sciences with only slight variation. Of course, up to the mid-20th century there were disagreements over what specific theoretical language to use in psychology. The major conflicts took place within so-called behavioristic or mechanistic schools that dominated psychology. Attempted inroads by Gestaltists and humanists were not considered serious threats, especially because they seemed to favor weakening, if not rejecting, the scientific method of conducting research through validation. The more relevant disagreements arose between schools of thought led by such psychological celebrities as Edward L. Thorndike, John B. Watson, Edward C. Tolman, B. F. Skinner, and Clark Hull. Thus, a graduate student of that period might study the essentials of a debate between "Skinnerians" versus "Hullians." And a thoughtful student might eventually realize that both of these schools supported the identical image of behavior, so that what they may have quibbled over in any dispute never resulted in any significant theoretical advances taking place. We might say that unification was quite high at this point in psychology's history—both in theory and method—at least in the academic context where the nature of human organisms was under detailed examination.

It should be noted that this relatively smooth unification occurred during a historical period that was moving from a strictly agricultural to a growing industrial emphasis (Bell, 1973). Machinery was the primary model adopted for the understanding of behavior in either higher or lower organisms. In the style of natural science, causation was pictured as involving *material* and *efficient* causation (from Aristotle, see Rychlak, 1994, pp. 7–8). This follows natural science description, in which characteristics of motion and action are without intention or willful choice. A rock, rolling down a hill, has no influence on its course—and the same is true of living human organisms walking down the hill. To capture teleological (intentional) behavior—in contradiction to mechanistic behavior—causation must be extended to the *formal* and *final* variety in which human beings are said to have the ability to evaluate their circumstances in life and willfully effect changes when called for (p. 8). Given the perception that psychology needs to attain natural science status in psychology, the shift in causal influence—from machine-like action to that of choice and intention—was not welcomed by the so-called tough-minded psychologists of the profession. As the modern and postmodern aspects of culture began making inroads on the profession of psychology in the closing decades of the 20th century, we saw rising expectations for both theory and method to embrace diversity. Diversity today is not something to be swallowed up by unity; it is something to be furthered, nourished, and protected in its own right (see Rychlak, 2003).

One of the professional groups to be identified as clearly different from "just" psychology was clinical psychology. I think this distinguishing of a branch of the profession to be something unique helped set the stage for the groups of specialists to follow, who sought recognition for their specialty in like manner. The global definition of being strictly a psychologist was gradually disregarded in preference for this seemingly more important title. Of course, clinicians did have to take additional preparation in the field, filling positions as interns in mental hospitals and so forth. The call for assistance by psychiatrists following World War II is what enabled this specialization in psychology to take place. The funding of training and subsequent employment opportunities made available by the U.S. Veterans Administration also played a major role (Humphreys, 1996). In time, clinical psychologists won the right to engage in psychotherapy. But it seems clear that much of the modeling for diversity in psychological specialties emanated from the experience of clinical psychology, with other specialties such as educational psychology and industrial psychology not far behind. The desire of psychologists to sort themselves into diverse divisions in the American Psychological Association (APA) was plainly evident and has persisted to this day.

UNIFYING PSYCHOLOGY VIA THEORY

An unfortunate outcome of identifying oneself with certain schools of thought in an effort to unify psychologists through such group formations is that exactly the opposite can take place. Each school is likely to have favored theoretical explanations that dismiss alternatives out of hand and permit only certain forms of experimental designs in the methodological pursuit of knowledge. Members of one group do not even make the effort to read and understand the positions taken by "outsiders" from another group, even though they may be investigating the same topic. This establishment of sides can never lead to a genuinely unified discipline. Robert J. Sternberg has analyzed this unfortunate state of affairs in great detail, arriving at the following insightful understanding of a unified psychology:

> Unified psychology . . . means giving up a single paradigm in favor of the use of whatever paradigm may help shed light on a problem. Multiple paradigms can contribute to the understanding of a single psychological phenomenon, whereas locking oneself into any single paradigm reduces one's ability to fully grasp the phenomenon of interest. (Sternberg & Grigorenko, 2001, p. 1077)

Although Sternberg does refer to certain strictures concerning methodological efforts, his main criticism appears to be on the side of theory. His examination of "method" concerns limiting rather than broadening the range of experimental designs. He is not analyzing anything like the validity of scientific method in the first place (something we will confront later). Thus he speaks critically of the tendency to place "exclusive or almost exclusive reliance on a single methodology (e.g., response–time measurements or fMRI measurements) rather than multiple converging methodologies for studying psychological phenomena" (Sternberg & Grigorenko, 2001, p. 1069). Sternberg referred to this latter strategy as "converging operations" (p. 1071). A similar meaning can be found in his discussion of theoretical paradigms, where he notes that in psychology there tends to be an unfortunate "adherence to single underlying paradigms for the investigation of psychological phenomena (e.g., behaviorism, cognitivism, psychoanalysis)" (p. 1069). It is not likely that advocates of behaviorism make reasoned efforts to understand psychoanalysis or vice versa. Yet a convergent effort to sincerely learn through another's—even an opponent's perspective—can be instructive and thereby help to intellectually unify the discipline of psychology. This is what I meant in an earlier paper by "unification through understanding and tolerance of opposition" (Rychlak, 1988). Too many psychologists ignore, if not actively repress, their opposition.

Sternberg finds serious problems arising when there is an "identification of scholars in psychology in terms of psychological subdisciplines (e.g., social psychology or clinical psychology) rather than in terms of the psychological phenomena they study" (Sternberg & Grigorenko, 2001, p. 1069). I have already suggested that such subdisciplines arose—at least in part—in an effort to attain prestige. Sternberg now points out that in their search for prestige such efforts to single out divisions merely promote the tendency to look narrowly at whatever (theoretical) topic is being investigated. Instead of focusing on the theoretical matter under study with a wide-ranging interest, we find an immediate narrowing in the sense of "There is a social–psychological way of handling this problem" or "There is a clinical–psychological way of handling this problem." Sternberg contends that it is better to consider one's professional self-image as that of a psychologist studying some problem rather than as a social psychologist, for example, committed to the use of shop-worn solutions. The latter attitude fails to encourage unifying growth in the discipline.

Another major contributor to the problems of unification in psychology is Arthur W. Staats (1991, 1999; Staats & Heiby, 1996). Like Sternberg, he also emphasizes theoretical rather than methodological aspects of unification. Staats is critical of early behaviorists for the effort they made to "defeat traditional psychology" (Staats & Heiby, 1996, p. 10), which sought "the perspective of human behavior study" (p. 5). Although Staats would not put it this way, I suggest that he is recognizing the disparity in causal analysis that academic psychology consistently ignores. The behaviorists opted for exclusive reliance on efficient causation (which is the way traditional science theorized), and the humanists were seeking to introduce theoretical concepts that ultimately relied on formal and final causation. Behaviorism ridiculed teleological theories of this stripe, and the refusal to integrate such contrasting points of view has come back to haunt psychology.

Staats (1991) noted that the era of grandeur in psychological theorizing is over. The problem in the past was that each theorist proposing concepts introduced new terms or interpreted older terminology in a new way. As a consequence, psychology lacked an infrastructure to make its ideas known in a uniform manner. Psychology needs to unify around a common theoretical language, with well-defined and universally understood meanings. For example, the word "self" has been used to mean self-esteem, self-image, self-concept, self-efficacy, and so forth. But what is the difference between self-image and self-concept or between self-esteem and self-efficacy? Psychology seems burdened with such nebulous comparisons. To build an infrastructure Staats suggested that an interfield theory must be devised as a kind of Rosetta-stone strategy in which multiple terminologies will be given an unequivocal meaning. This clarity will promote unification. Staats called this approach "unification psychology" (Staats, 1991, p. 899). And since the common understanding can be proven through empirical methodological testing, he spoke of a "unified positivism" as well (p. 899).

So we have an interesting contrast of suggestions for unification through theoretical considerations. Sternberg's approach calls for the broadening of theoretical scope, encouraging psychologists to pay attention to a wider array of useful ideas and, in this way, even when they disagree with certain points of view they will at least understand them rather than ignore them. And, of course, it is also possible for any theorist to modify his or her understanding thanks to such widening of perspectives. At the very least, psychologists will be acknowledging that explanations of human nature are not easily captured, and because no one can honestly be said to have the "one and only" account on this matter, a pecking order will no longer be viable. Staats, on the other hand, thinks it is necessary to reduce the range of commentary by finding a uniform terminology. He acknowledges the mistakes made by earlier behavioristic theorists, who did not give humanism a chance to develop. Based on his writings, I have the impression that he still believes a kind of modern behaviorism (i.e., unified positivism) will be capable of subsuming such humanistic explanations after all. In other words, he has hopes of subsuming a teleological humanistic account by a mechanistic account. This would require subsuming formal and final causation by material and efficient causation. I do not believe this is possible, even though I fully understand Staats's motives for harboring such dreams. Once psychologists begin conducting empirical experiments they invariably cast their independent–dependent variables as efficiently caused sequences, with the former thrusting the latter in a mechanistic fashion. Because humanists view human beings as self-directing and not mechanical robots, there is just no way to make this kind of theorizing plausible. We need to take a broader sweep of what is involved, in the style of Sternberg. But there is still an extremely important problem regarding the scientific method that we must consider.

UNIFYING PSYCHOLOGY VIA METHOD

There has been a significant development taking place in psychology, originating in the 1960s and becoming acute in the 1990s. I refer to a growing attack on the traditional scientific method of validation. Many analysts have pointed to a growing influence of the postmodern world view in this attack. As one expert summarized things: "Post-modern social science presumes methods that multiply paradox, inventing ever more elaborate repertoires of questions, each of which encourages an infinity of answers, rather than methods that settle on solutions" (Rosenau, 1992, p. 117). The elaboration of repertoires stems from the heavy use of "dialogue," in which there is a continuing "arm chair" pursuit of answers to questions raised in the verbal exchange. Because, as I noted earlier, science never establishes certainty in its experimental results (i.e., alternative interpretations can always occur), the postmodern advocate takes this to mean that the method used is fatally flawed. Thus, "as far as method is concerned, 'anything goes' " (Rosenau, 1992, p. 117).

My colleagues and I have traced a steady decline in the support given to traditional empirical validation over the last decade of the 20th century. An increasing number of psychologists questioned whether their specialty was meant to be a "true" science in the sense of pursuing empirical evidence for all of its involvements. Feelings and convictions were considered more important than proven facts. Students at some universities resisted the study of advanced statistics because they claimed it had little to do with their daily work as clinicians. The same was said of having to learn experimental research design. Students petitioned to take nonexperimental graduate degrees because they failed to see the merit of such preparation for careers in a "helping profession." It is almost as if the great acceptance of psychology in the general culture, where today virtually everyone uses psychological lingo and offers psychic explanations of emotional problems, has crystallized psychology into a helping profession and no more. When I attended graduate school in the 1950s, we were taught to be scientists first and clinical psychologists second. The picture is quite different today. This decline in scientific commitment is cause for considerable worry over the future of psychology as a scientific profession. Gardner (1992) has suggested that psychology has become so fragmented that it may lose much of its constituency to other fields such as cognitive neuroscience. Others have noted that, in its rush to become a "helping" profession rather than a science, psychology seems to be giving itself over to biology in one form or another.

What is to be done in all of this? Howard W. Kendler, who has written considerably on the deterioration of science in psychology, had this to say:

> It is difficult to understand how the proponents of a so-called unified psychology can ignore basic and irreconcilable methodological conflicts that permeate contemporary psychology. (2002, p. 1125)

How indeed! I must admit that this question of just what constitutes valid assessment strikes me as the most important problem facing psychology. If psychology rejects the scientific method it rejects its scientific status—a catastrophe that I shudder to think about. Kendler (1970) has suggested that there is a natural division between psychology as a natural science on the one hand and as a social science on the other. He faults the social science aspect of the profession for current problems, and one could make a strong argument in his defense. Basically, he is a reductionist who would have psychology dealing exclusively in material and efficient causation. One of his papers carried the title of "A Good Divorce Is Better Than a Bad Marriage" (Kendler, 1987). In it he argued that an amicable divorce between mechanistic and teleological formulations makes more sense than trying to live on under a continued maladaptive state of tension. If a split occurs, the assumption is that there at least would be unity in two separate camps. Kendler has the old-fashioned attitude that Staats referred to, of wanting the humanistic types in psychology to "go away," allowing the "real" psychological scientists to do their work unfettered with postmodern romantic nonsense and political scheming.

The only possible unification is within the ends of a split—humanists on the one side and mechanists on the other. Of course, one cannot even be certain about this alignment, because there are always the disagreements within the sides to consider. If things were as easy to separate as Kendler suggested, we probably would have witnessed a far more successful adaptation in psychology than we have to date. In effect, Kendler's critical assessment strikes me as a continuation of the complaints leveled by earlier psychologists who were trying to keep humanistic theory out of circulation in the discipline. Even though I agree that there is much nonsense permeating the science of psychology at present, I do not think this situation will persist. Some adjustments have to be made and I suspect that we will have to live through a period in which postmodern formulations run their course. Let us hope that we can outlive this difficult period without tearing our profession in two.

IN HOPES OF A UNIFIED PSYCHOLOGY

I would now like to pull together the views presented earlier in an effort to clearly state the kind of unification psychology should be pursuing. The first point to make is that we are not seeking unification to simplify or "dummy down" our profession. Nor do we want a unity in which psychologists are expected to blindly support a "party line." Unity is not conformity. Bunching psychologists into "schools" that seek to repress the ideas of other schools is not the way to behave in a mature science. Recall that the period of roughly 1930 to 1970 became the era of competing in such schools, each strategizing to do the other in by way of empirical tests that were required to describe findings via a received view (essentially, a behavioristic account). The 1970s and especially the 1980s brought computer explanation into the field, and this rapidly overtook the earlier schools thanks to the fact that the efficient-cause theoretical way of explaining things was left untouched. The old "stimulus–response and mediation" theoretical formulation became the new "input–output and feedback" theoretical formulation. Nothing had really changed in the image of humanity being advanced. Difficult issues such as the matter of theorizing about human agency, choice, and free will continued to be discredited as something other than a genuinely scientific line of inquiry. Kendler (2002) referred to such teleological explanations as "romantic" formulations unable to absorb "realistic" views of human behavior. It is this kind of disunity that we seek to correct.

I think that Staats had a good point to make in his suggestion that psychology needs an infrastructure in its use of terminology. However, I would take this suggestion in another direction. I believe that all graduate students in psychology should be given an in-depth course in the history of science, so that they develop a sophisticated understanding of just what is involved in doing science. Unfortunately, I have found that what they learn about scientific theorizing and the empirical testing of scientific research is more likely to result in a fear-based hatred of science than a genuine understanding of what is involved. One of the common erroneous notions students often gather from superficial coverage in other courses is that traditional natural science can be applied only to a mechanistic theory, so there is no hope for examining the more teleological aspects of the human being. This ignorance arises because of a frequently encountered confound in psychological writings between theory and method. This error occurs when the stimulus–response theoretical sequence is identified with the independent–dependent variable methodological sequence. In other words, just as the stimulus is said to efficiently cause the response to be triggered or thrust along like colliding billiard balls, so too the independent variable efficiently causes the dependent variable to come about (be shaped, etc.). This erroneous equation is true only in the minds of mechanists who have not been given a sophisticated account of the scientific method. The scientific method would obviously lose its objectivity if it were to dictate the theories being put to test in its use. Science would be out the window. I do not think that Kendler's division between natural and social sciences means any more than this—one side (mechanists) has been taught to think only in efficient-cause terminology and the other side (teleologists) has not been taught how to argue back when critics refer to its members as "romantics."

So what we have achieved in teaching our students science is the broad background from which everyone can draw a common understanding. This desire for more breadth is clearly implied in Sternberg's approach to unification. The language system used by psychologists will be clarified and made familiar to all. In his unified positivism, Staats (1999) argued that underlying the many topics studied in psychology there are common principles, and that in having these common principles clarified psychologists would have a basis for making better sense of what their work entails. Psychologists in time would come to realize that their ideas are often not terribly different from their peers. I have my doubts that such commonality in ideas would necessarily be identified (observed, etc.) empirically. I think we have a purely theoretical question, a way of thinking about our ideas even before we put them to empirical test. These are arbitrary notions, put forward in hopes of being instructive. In seeing our colleague's theory more clearly I think a spirit of mutual acceptance will be more likely to develop. This is kind of like the old saw of walking about for a time in another's shoes. This strolling about promotes empathic understanding. I think the name calling will diminish and maybe end altogether once such empathy matures into tolerance.

Of course, there is still the nagging issue over whether or not psychology is actually a science. I cannot help but wonder how the denigration of teleological theorizing in psychology helped to develop this damaging point of view. I mean that it is probably more likely for someone to challenge the scientific status of psychology following a series of "put-downs" by self-styled "real" scientists in the Kendler mold. This is obviously a defensive maneuver by the rejected person, to win the freedom to study humanistic topics by challenging the very scientific basis of our profession. But I do think this takes place, and greater unity among psychologists should help solve the problem. Another reason I think we have this situation today is that so many of our entering students come into the area of study with the applied bias that I mentioned earlier. This gets furthered as educational levels progress. Such students are not motivated by scientific curiosity. At this point we could easily take up an analysis of the actual scientific interest of many faculty members in departments of psychology. I think that psychology is a complex subject to pursue. Because of its complexity it can be removed from the realm of science and still find many other avenues in which to pursue its interests. Psychology can be kept alive many different ways. Even so, I personally hope and trust that it will remain a science.

REFERENCES

Bell, D. (1973). *The coming of post-industrial society: A venture in social forecasting.* New York: Basic Books.

Gardner, H. (1992). Scientific psychology: Should we bury it or praise it? *New Ideas in Psychology, 10,* 179–190.

Humphreys, K. (1996). Clinical psychologists as psychotherapists: History, future, and alternatives. *American Psychologist, 51,* 190–197.

Kendler, H. W. (1970). The unity of psychology. *Canadian Psychologist, 11,* 30–47.

Kendler, H. W. (1987). A good divorce is better than a bad marriage. In A. W. Staats & L. P. Mos (Eds.), *Annals of theoretical psychology* (Vol. 5, pp. 55–89). New York: Plenum Press.

Kendler, H. W. (2002). Romantic versus realistic views of psychology. *American Psychologist, 57,* 1125–1126.

Palter, R. (1956). Philosophic principles and scientific theory. *Philosophy of Science, 23,* 111–135.

Rosenau, P. M. (1992). *Post-modernism and the social sciences: Insights, inroads, and intrusions.* Princeton, NJ: Princeton University Press.

Rychlak, J. F. (1980). The false promise of falsification. *Journal of Mind and Behavior, 1,* 183–195.

Rychlak, J. F. (1988). Unification through understanding and tolerance of opposition. *International Newsletter of Uninomic Psychology, 5,* 13–15.

Rychlak, J. F. (1994). *Logical learning theory: A human teleology and its empirical support.* Lincoln: University of Nebraska Press.

Rychlak, J. F. (2003). *The human image in postmodern America.* Washington, DC: American Psychological Association.

Staats, A. W. (1991). Unified positivism and unification psychology: Fad or new field? *American Psychologist, 46,* 899–912.

Staats, A. W. (1999). Unifying psychology requires new infrastructure, theory, method, and a research agenda. *Review of General Psychology, 3,* 3–13.

Staats, A. W., & Heiby, E. M. (1996). Psychological behaviorism: Vehicle for the third generation of behavior therapy/analysis. *International Newsletter of Uninomic Psychology, 16,* 3–11.

Sternberg, R. J., & Grigorenko, E. L. (2001). Unified psychology. *American Psychologist, 56,* 1069–1079.

Yanchar, S. C., & Slife, B. D. (2000). The problematic of fragmentation: A hermaneutic proposal. *Journal of Mind and Behavior, 21,* 235–242.

10

A ROAD TO, AND PHILOSOPHY OF, UNIFICATION

ARTHUR W. STAATS

Identifying as an experimental psychologist, I have always been motivated to advance acceptance of psychology as a science. Although not usually announced, furthering acceptance of psychology as a science has been a goal of scientific psychologists, especially experimental psychologists, since the science began. Within that context it is traitorous to suggest that our field is less than a science. I would not do that, because my firm conviction is that psychology *is* a science. But I cannot add *in every sense of the word*. Let me explain, because this subtlety has led to some confusion (see Driver-Linn, 2003).

Although experimental psychologists proclaim the field is a science, there is disbelief among many others who consider that psychology as a behavioral–social science is fundamentally, inherently different from and less than the physical, chemical, and biological sciences. Psychology may be accorded the name of science and have a place in society as a science and receive support as a science. Yet the belief that psychology is less than a true science affects its status, the support it is accorded, and the acceptance of its products. Those of us who are scientific psychologists want psychology to be a full science, and to be accepted as such. It would be important for these reasons, as well as reasons internal to the progress of the science itself, to clarify the nature of the difference between psychology and fully accepted sciences such as physics. If our science has frailties that need fixing this must be recognized so that development can begin. As I indicate, it is in this framework that my interest in psychology's unity arose.

FROM UNIFIED THEORY TO THE PROBLEM OF UNIFICATION

I became a behaviorist in 1953 through reading Clark Hull and Kenneth Spence and other logical–positivist views of science and psychology as a science (for example, Stevens, 1951). I took my PhD in general–experimental but also completed the requirements for a clinical degree, including a VA internship, because unlike the animal-focused behaviorism of that time my interest focused on functional human behavior of concern to various fields of psychology. Although not analyzing this at the time, my goal also demanded development of a basic learning–behavior theory for dealing broadly with human behavior and its problems.

Actually, Watson (1930) originally projected his behaviorism as a grand theory that should replace the traditional approach to psychology. This tradition was followed in the second generation. Hull stated in the preface to his 1943 book his belief that his theory would apply generally to human behavior. Followers took the same position (e.g., Dollard & Miller, 1950; Doob, 1948; Maltzman, 1955; Osgood, 1953). Within this general framework many laboratory demonstrations of learning principles with human research participants were conducted (for example, Cofer & Foley, 1942; Deese, 1959; Russell & Storms, 1955). Skinner's radical behaviorism (1953, 1957) also projected his experimental analysis of behavior technology (his operant conditioning apparatus) as the methodology with which to study human behavior (see Bijou, 1957; Lindsley, 1956).

It is important to note that the fundamental assumption of these behavioristic approaches was that the basic animal learning principles were sufficient to account generally for human behavior. But behaviorism actually had no program for studying the types of human behavior of concern to the various fields of psychology, clinical psychology, educational psychology, abnormal psychology, psychological measurement, child psychology, and personality. Behaviorism's goal was that of basic science—a projection that in some future development the basic principles could be applied. Behaviorism, thus, had no program for unifying the products and concerns of behaviorism with the products and concerns of nonbehavioral psychology. So behaviorism, like the other approaches, actually had no understanding of psychology's character with respect to unity or disunity, or of any special problems or needs psychology might have in this area.

In fact behaviorism displayed the same ways of operating with respect to unity as did nonbehavioral psychology, and thus contributed in the usual way to psychology's problem of disunity. For example, although there was great commonality among the major behaviorism theories (such as those of Clark Hull, Edward Tolman, and B. F. Skinner), the theories were set forth as separate, independent, and different. No effort was expended in abstracting that which was common to the theories, setting it aside as consensual, and then proceeding in working with that which was different toward the goal of creating a unified body of knowledge.

Although my theory (Staats, 1963) began in the behaviorism tradition, it did not follow behaviorism characteristics in various ways, including disinterest in constructing unified knowledge. Watson's program was to *replace* traditional psychology with behaviorism. That position was carried over into radical behaviorism and largely into the other variants of behaviorism. What I came to call psychological behaviorism (see Tryon, 1990), however, widely analyzed nonbehavioral products of psychology in terms of learning–behavioral principles.

> Specifically, "broadening" and integration of learning and attitude theory must include extension into areas involving the same events— whether or not these areas have traditionally been considered within the study of attitudes, or whether the terminology or research methods are the same as those customary in the study of attitudes. The use of different terms and methods are accidents of history which prevent us from seeing commonality in underlying principles. We need theory that shows the common principles and thereby helps unify the study of human behavior. (Staats, 1968, p. 34)

Each such analysis was a unification across opposed areas (for example, learning theory and personality theory), across methods (for example, behavioral research and psychological test construction), across basic and applied science (for example, in joining clinical and child-educational phenomena with learning–behavior principles in helping found the fields of behavior therapy and behavior analysis), and across normal and abnormal (for example, making learning–behavior analyses of behavior disorders; see Staats, 1963).

Besides what this unification work taught me in terms of constructing unified theory, the work and its products also formed a new type of "lens" for examining our field. That lens induced me to look at psychology's operation and products from the standpoint of unification. Early on I began to see that psychology had some odd characteristics with respect to unity, characteristics that were not part of the models of science derived from the older physical sciences. I have already mentioned psychology's disinterest in examining the major behaviorisms from the standpoint of the large commonality they had. There were other indications of lack of concern with unification. For example, Hull (1920) used the idea of *concept formation* and Skinner (1953) used the idea of *abstraction*. I noted similar examples in the terms *instrumental conditioning* and *operant conditioning, classical conditioning,* and *respondent conditioning,* and many other pairs that shared the same empirical meanings. Moreover, such redundancy occurred in every area of psychology. The unity lens, comparing the model sciences to psychology, showed a huge discrepancy that went unnoticed in psychology. Because the model sciences would never allow redundancy of concepts. The concept of *electron,* for example, could not be given different names when used in different theories. However, I saw that psychology was filled with redundancy, artificial diversity that complicates the science immeasurably, with no sign anything unusual or disadvantageous was recognized. There was no attempt to remove redundancy, whereas in the model sciences there are explicit instructions on how different elements in theories, that are actually the same, can be reduced to one (see Nagel, 1961, chap. 11).

It was astounding to me that such a discrepancy could exist in our discipline, striving with all its might to be recognized as a science. I first raised the question of psychology's "separatism" and need for unification in the 1960s (see Staats, 1968, 1970).

> The history of psychology is a history of separatism of various types; for example, learning versus cognitive approaches. Moreover, major efforts within traditional learning approaches have been expended in developing and maintaining separate experimental methods, separate general (philosophical) methodologies, and separate terminologies. . . . [W]e have categories like problem solving, perception, communication, personality, word meaning, imitation, intelligence, motivation, social interaction, and so on, as though there was in each case a unitary process involved. The investigations of these various types of behavior have proceeded also in isolation from one another—even though it may be suggested that the same principles underlie the various behavioral events. . . . This is very disadvantageous. . . . (Staats, 1968, p. 33)

It became ever more clear that in the area of disunity–unity psychology had a different character than the older, more accepted sciences. The general problem of disunity came progressively to define a major interest for me (see Staats, 1970, 1975, 1981, 1983, 1987, 1991, 1996, 1999). In 1983 I organized an American Psychological Association (APA) convention symposium on psychology's disunity with Sigmund Koch and Howard Kendler, both pro, and I con, with Gregory Kimble as the discussant. (We joked at the time that we participants outnumbered the audience.) The next year my attempt to begin a group interested in unity yielded only four other interested parties (Cyril Franks, Leonard Burns, Leonard Krasner, and Albert Gilgen). We met, however, and decided to organize APA convention talks and symposia and to begin a newsletter (that I edited) as a prelude to forming an organization on disunity–unity. Building on our progress, the next year we had a much larger group and formed the Society for the Study of Unity Issues in Psychology. In the next decade we annually organized APA events on this topic (and these were presented in the newsletter). Almost entirely the various works produced dealt with the pros and cons of unification. Some took positions that diversity was good in science, that psychology was no different than other sciences. Some took the position that psychology had a special problem of disunity. Highlighting psychology's problem of disunity also motivated new formulations of general schemes aiming at unification (Boneau, 1988; Kimble, 1997).

The same year that I organized that first APA symposium on psychology's disunity–unity I published a book on psychology's "crisis of disunity" (Staats, 1983) in which I described psychology's problem of disunity.

THE "WOULD-BE" SCIENCE

In this book I marshaled evidence that psychology had a critical problem that was impeding its development as a science and impeding being accepted as a science. The symptoms of the problem were evident to those, such as the philosopher of science Steven Toulmin, who study sciences.

> The characteristic features of *would-be disciplines* can best be illustrated . . . [when] we turn to professional psychologists [and other social scientists] for explanation of the behavior of individual human beings. . . . [W]e find a diversity of approaches of a kind unparalleled in physics. . . . [a] split into parties, factions, or sects, which have not managed to hammer out a common set of disciplinary goals. . . . So long as *would-be disciplines* remain in this inchoate condition, no agreed family of fundamental concepts or constellation of basic presuppositions . . . can establish itself with authority. (Toulmin, 1972, pp. 380–382, italics added)

Toulmin was able to see that something was awry in psychology (and the other behavioral or social sciences). He could even describe some of the specific characteristics that are different from those in the "real sciences." But, without an explanatory framework, the natural tendency is to conclude that this difference must be inherent in psychology, that psychology is just different, defective, basically unable to produce the character of real science. Essentially the same belief is held by many psychologists (see Koch, 1981) who are convinced that psychology has peculiarities that prevent it from ever being a science. In a nutshell, it is frequently said in various ways that there are two kinds of science, hard science and soft science, real science and would-be science, science and social science, and such. I did not like that view and my efforts to understand what is involved in the differences between psychology and physical science gave me a means by which to reject that view.

EARLY SCIENCE CHARACTERISTICS

Central to resolving the puzzle was explanation of how psychology could be a real science if it had characteristics that differ so much from those of real science. A first step that my unity lens revealed was that the philosophy, history, and sociology of science did not deal systematically with the differences between sciences like physics and psychology along with the consideration of the natures of early and mature sciences. However, there were descriptions of science here and there that could be pieced together in providing an explanation and resolving the puzzle.

> [During the first half of the eighteenth century] there were almost as many views about the nature of electricity as there were important electrical experimenters. . . . [A]ll were components of real scientific theories drawn from experiment and observation. . . . [However, there was general divisiveness, leading to unguided fact gathering, and this] produces a morass. (Kuhn, 1962, pp. 13–15)

As many views as there were experimenters, general divisiveness, unguided fact gathering, a morass of knowledge? Whoa! These are not descriptions of physical science as we know it, or of the products of such science. These descriptions of early physical science are like my descriptions of psychology's separatism and disunity and like Toulmin's descriptions of psychology as a would-be science.

I saw deep meaning in the description of the products of early physics as a morass of diversity. This suggested that early physicists were interested in constructing their own separate theories, not in constructing a unified body of knowledge. We might infer those scientists had no conviction that the different phenomena they studied had any underlying commonality. We can also see a characteristic of the operation of early science in the sociology of science descriptions of the battles early physical scientists had over who discovered what. Galileo was described as a "seasoned campaigner" in defending his priority of discovery in various areas against various other claimants.

> The peerless Newton fought several battles with Robert Hooke over priority in optics and celestial mechanics and entered into a long and painful controversy with Leibnitz over the invention of the calculus. Hook, who has been described as the "universal claimant" because "there was scarcely a discovery in his time which he did not conceive

himself to claim (and, it might be added, often justly so, for he was one of the most inventive men in his century of genius). (Merton, 1957, pp. 635–636)

Cavendish, Watt, Lavoisier, Jenner, Lister, Faraday, Wollaston, and Davy are names of other prominent early scientists involved in such contests. "Laplace, several of the Bernoullis, Legendre, Gauss, and Cauchy were only a few of the giants among mathematicians embroiled in quarrels over priority" (Merton, 1957, p. 636). These descriptions indicated that this manner of operation continued for a long time.

> The case of the great mathematician Cauchy was even more notorious. On receiving a paper for refereeing, he could not resist the temptation of recasting the proof, improving the result, developing and generalizing it in all sorts of ways, and finally publishing it in a journal to which he had rapid access. When the paper which had originally stimulated him finally appear in print, it would seem singularly crude and pointless in comparison to the results already published by the master. (Ravetz, 1971, p. 256)

We can see from these examples that rather than being rare occasions, these were part of the operating fabric of early physical science. Prominent scientists behaved in this manner, and their success indicates the practices did not result in being drummed from the corps.

What effect did this operational characteristic have on the science? Communication has been called the life-blood of science, because science advances in a building way, progressive steps becoming possible when earlier steps have been taken. For that to occur expeditiously, of course, it is necessary that avenues of communication be open. Those avenues were compromised by the fact that in early physics there were no established procedures for preventing theft of the discovery by others. One mechanism of protection of one's intellectual property was to announce it to various people at the same time, but in anagrammatic form so the finding could not be understood. That would arouse attention and interest and establish ownership and time of discovery. Then, in due time, the discovery could be presented in understandable form.

> Galileo used this method, and Kepler tried unsuccessfully to decipher his anagrammatic announcement of the discovery of the non-spherical appearance of Saturn. Other users include Hooke, Huygens, and Newton himself. . . . From the difficulties they had, we can see that a significant proportion of the great "scientists" of that age were even more concerned by the protection of their intellectual property, than for an immediate realization of its value through the prestige resulting from publication, to say nothing of contributing to the co-operative endeavour. (Ravetz, 1971, p. 249)

Very clearly the operation of the science was aberrant by today's standards of operation. Why did they behave that way? The answer is that the operation of early science lacked formal means for protection of the intellectual property of the scientist. With no "sociological" system that guaranteed safety of intellectual property it was necessary for the individual scientist to concoct ways of attaining credit for discovery. Today the situation is far different.

> There are formal and informal sanctions for failure to refer to other research. The informal sanctions involve those scientists who earn a reputation for non-reference, a reputation that travels by word of mouth. ... [With respect to] formal sanction ... [i]f referees, editors, or the injured party know a paper has not referred to the relevant research, the first two may require it before publication while the latter may lodge a complaint to the editor and cause the publication to carry proper citation. (Gaston, 1973, p. 114)

THE UNITY–DISUNITY DIMENSION

These descriptions of early physics and mathematics do not seem like science as we know it. If Stephen Toulmin, the philosopher of science, were to describe early physical science—both in its products and in its way of operating—he would have to call it "would-be" science. And all this leads to my premise: There is a dimension in the advancement of science that has not been recognized and dealt with systematically. The dimension is that of disunity–unity. *Sciences begin in disunity and they progress toward unification. In that process they change in various fundamental characteristics, characteristics of operation, of product, of goals, of view of the world, and of values.*

I have already given examples of the manner in which early physics and contemporary physics differ in their operation and product. Let me suggest that goals also change as the science progresses toward unity. For example, the goal of early science is the discovery of something new. That includes discovering new phenomena, for example, a new star. It includes developing a new apparatus for observing phenomena, for example, stars. It includes also formulating a new theory, for example, concerning what stars are and what their origin is. Discovery of the novel is pretty much the major goal of early science. Later, however, additional achievements become recognized as important. For example, Shapere (1979) presented examples in which we can see the emergence of a new type knowledge, that of *relationships among discoveries.*

> Thus there were strong grounds for believing electricity and magnetism constituted distinct subjects for investigation, for which different

explanations were to be given. Nevertheless, in spite of these clear differences, reasons accumulated over the succeeding two or three centuries for *suspecting* that these differences might prove to be superficial, and that there was some deep relationship to be found between electrical and magnetic phenomena. (Shapere, 1977, pp. 519)

Shapere also described how electricity and chemical phenomena, first considered as entirely different, come to be considered as possibly related, and then specifically so. He does the same for electricity and light and finally for the relationship of all three, electricity, light, and magnetism. "Faraday's demonstration of the effect of a magnetic field on the plane of polarization of a light ray provided one sort of consideration leading to the belief that there was a deeper relationship to be sought between magnetism and light and hence, because of the developments summarized above, electricity and light" (Shapere, 1977, p. 521).

I would like to point out that considering the formulation of relationships between phenomena to be a new type of knowledge changes the fundamental nature of the science. When the finding of novel phenomena has been considered the only type of discovery in a science, the only goal of science is the finding of such novelty. But when finding relationships among phenomena has been shown to be valuable, then this introduces a new goal to the science. Looking for those relationships comes to be a valued activity. After a sufficient number of successes in finding such relationships has occurred, looking for such relationships becomes an important part of the mission of science.

That same development changes the scientist's view of the world. The scientist in early, "preunified" science—where the only goal is the development of a new and independent discovery—views the world as made up of different and independent phenomena. On the other hand, the scientist in the "unified" science—where there has already been much finding of relationships among phenomena formerly considered different—views the world as made up of various phenomena that are related and that can be explained by common underlying principles. These involve the two very different world views.

This difference in views is accompanied by a change in values and in the scientists' skills. The preunified science, because it considers only discovery of novelty as valuable, trains its scientists to look for novelty and to enhance the novelty of findings, and they become skilled at enhancing the novelty of their work. That involves gaining skill in showing how one's findings differ from other findings. The scientist is not trained in how to recognize similarity and relatedness and consequently does not become skillful in seeing them and in working to find them. The science is not set up to reward findings of similarity and relatedness, because finding them reduces the value of the novelty that is the one recognized type of scientific knowledge.

I am thus suggesting that in various ways there are deep differences between unified sciences and preunified sciences. Those differences are deep enough and important enough that, even without systematic definition, they are part of the differentiation between "real" and "would-be" sciences. Such a characterization implies that there are inherent qualities that make it impossible for a science such as that of psychology to ever become a full science. In contrast, I am suggesting that the two types of science differ on the extent of their development of unification: *All sciences begin in the preunified state and only over a long time develop to the unified state.*

In this regard it should be noted that Shapere describes the centuries of development involved in unifying the phenomena of electricity, magnetism, and light. My experience in 50 years of working on a unified theory tells me that psychology has the potential for becoming a unified science, as I began indicating more than 30 years ago (see also Staats, 1970). Nevertheless, this continues to be a projection on which not much progress has been made, so it may be said to be still in question. From the example of physics we might project a long time will be involved in psychology becoming a full, unified science.

THE MODERN PREUNIFIED SCIENCE

A fundamental difference in science concerns unification. In that respect, when taken from the beginning of the particular science, all sciences are alike. They all begin without unification. That does not mean, however, that they all have the same problems in becoming unified sciences. To illustrate, when physics began as a science there were few scientists, the methodology of science was not well understood, there were few pieces of apparatus, science had yet to be defined as a social institution to be allocated the financial support of society, and the phenomena to be studied were limited in number. Because of such factors the production of scientific knowledge was limited. So one scientist could encompass all that was known of physics.

Contrast that with today. There are thousands of physicists, there is a huge range of phenomena to study, there is great development of the apparatus and methodology by which to conduct that study, and there is huge support of society for that study. As a consequence the outpouring of knowledge is a deluge. No longer can the single scientist encompass that which is known in physics. There is a huge difference in these "material" characteristics of science.

My point is that the struggle of the preunified science to become unified is affected by such "material" characteristics of science. To illustrate that impact, take children's picture puzzles. A primary dimension of difficulty resides in the number of pieces of a puzzle. The greater the number of pieces the more difficult the puzzle. The same is true of unification. The greater the number of pieces to be put together, the greater the task of unifying a science. When there are few phenomena, apparatuses, scientists, and support for research, few pieces of knowledge are produced and the task of unification is easier than when the material features of a science result in producing a great many pieces of knowledge.

A problem of the preunified science of psychology is that it is a modern science materially. It has many scientists, and they are well supported by society. Psychology has a well-developed methodology, many apparatuses, many phenomena to study, and many sources of publication of research findings. These material characteristics guarantee that psychology produces a huge number of pieces of knowledge. Psychology is a modern preunified science and, anomalously, this is a drawback, because its greater production of knowledge makes its problems of unification far greater than was the case for physics. Physics was fortunate to go through its unifying foundation before the time when it became enormously productive. Moreover, psychology's production of knowledge units will only grow, which guarantees continued production of pieces of knowledge that, other things equal, all make the task of unification more and more difficult.

Psychology's Preunified Science Characteristics

Human behavior is complex, and psychology has a limitless number of phenomena of interest to study. Because of the nature of the preunified science, those who study the phenomena are not instructed to look for relationships to other phenomena or how to find such relationships. This is true even when the phenomena on superficial consideration might be considered to be closely related. As a simple example, take phenomena such as interests, values, motivation, emotion, attitudes, needs, hedonic valence, evaluative meaning, and mood. There are many study areas that deal with these phenomena, or facets of these phenomena. The studies are largely done in isolation from one another, however, despite the apparent relationships. Those working in each area do not seek theory unifications that would draw such phenomena together, establish their common underlying principles, and thereby explain them in a unified framework. There are innumerable phenomena in psychology that exist in such solitude. Cognitive psychology, for example, has them in great supply, across different fields of psychology. Many believe they are working in a unified cognitive psychology because they use cognitive terms for the phenomena in which they are interested. But that is not the case. The many "cognitive" studies are not derived from any common underlying theory. Cognitive psychologists in social, developmental, clinical, experimental, and educational psychology do not draw from any set of common underlying principles and do not interrelate their works. What is done in one area of "cognitive" research does not advance other areas. None are considered basic to the others. There is little use of the cognitive psychology of "basic" experimental psychology from which to draw concepts and principles for applied developments. It turns out that the only relationship among fields and research areas is the loose belief that they are cognitive phenomena.

Added to the fact that there are many different phenomena in psychology, there are different methods of study used and different types of "apparatus." There are psychological tests, apparatuses for studying learning, brain imaging methods, clinical and naturalistic observations. Different theories are composed to address the same phenomena based on the use of different study methods, or based on studying different facets of the phenomena, or based on using a different theory language. Given the number of phenomena and their different facets, the number of different methods, the number of different theory languages, the number of islands of knowledge produced is limitless.

The great number of these islands of knowledge makes for difficulty in finding relationships. The large number of studies means a large number of journals and books. So the individual scientist can really only be expert in a small part of the knowledge of the science. (Mercifully, physics was launched in its unified development before it developed many specialized fields.) Perforce psychologists are generally specialists. This itself makes for redundancy. It is as though each scientist starts from scratch. Without an understanding of the need for work to connect and unify, the single goal of novelty actually produces artificial diversity. The value of one's effort is increased if it is novel, and novelty is the only goal. That framework motivates scientists to emphasize difference, not relatedness. One result is the redundancy that has already been described that amplifies greatly the science's chaos. The renaming of concepts, methods, principles, phenomena, and other science products is a common practice that goes unchallenged, although the practice is antithetical to the cohesiveness, parsimony, and nonredundancy of science.

There are many cases in psychology where something is set forth at the beginning and it is the only one. Let us consider Freud's theory as the starting point. There were those who built on that theory. But the same concepts, renamed and considered as different and independent, have been used in many different theories. In such cases rather than making progress in developing a unified body of knowledge such developments have produced greater diversity, contributing to more complex and unrelated knowledge.

Scientific rivalry is given carte blanche in the preunified science of psychology, however, by having no standards for the introduction of theory terms. Anyone can set forth a new theory, and whether or not the theory includes redundant concepts, principles, or empirical data is not considered. That is a preunified science way of operating. This makes for progress in a backward direction, producing a more and more diverse body of knowledge in which it is more and more difficult to attain simplicity, cohesion, and general meaning.

The unified science does not operate that way; a quark is a quark is a quark. If a physicist renamed a quark on including the phenomenon in a new theory, this would not be accepted. Unity of language, of course, is an important part of parsimony, a recognized goal of science. It is a tremendous advantage to a science—for the student, the researcher, or the applied scientist—to have only one theory language versus many. The existence of a large number of redundant terms in psychology within the many different and usually competitive theory languages is a huge handicap—a feature that differentiates the preunified science from the unified sciences. In part because there are no standards in psychology, it is not possible to learn even a fraction of the different theory languages in psychology. How much more effective is physics because the scientist has to learn only one basic language.

My major point is that psychology as a science has huge purview of phenomena. That guarantees that the puzzle of putting psychology together will be a huge task. When this is made even more difficult because of the operational characteristics of our science that create artificial diversity, the difficulty of the task is magnified greatly. These characteristics shape the science. The presence of great redundancy sets the stage for producing more redundancy simply out of ignorance of existing similarity. Moreover, because difference is accepted and expected, the science does not devote some portion of its resources to finding redundant concepts, principles, and theories in a concerted effort toward parsimony.

Shapere described how, over a period of hundreds of years, physics found commonality of underlying principles for electricity, magnetism, and light. This type of achievement has not occurred in psychology. Without a model to follow there is no effort being made toward such achievements. There are so many examples to illustrate. Take the field of personality theory. There are many theories. Nagel (1961) in characterizing science indicated that theories may have common elements and that this calls for "reduction"—that is, the reduction of like principles and concepts in two theories to singularity. But in psychology these principles of science operation do not apply; there is no systematic attempt to interrelate various theories. Do two theories contain some common elements? Do the theories examine the same phenomena or different phenomena? Are two theories differentiated because they use different methods even though they deal with the same phenomena? Are common elements treated as different because they are in different theories? Could knowledge be made parsimonious by accumulating their common elements and distinguishing their differences? As a specific example, could an overarching theory of personality be constructed that incorporated elements from the various personality theories? But the science does not instruct psychological scientists to work on answering such questions toward establishing relationships. Areas of study can spring up, have a flurry of activity, and disappear into the archives without anyone trying to establish any general meaning to the endeavor. Over a number of years a large portion of experimental psychology was devoted to the study of verbal learning and memory, with thousands of studies disappearing into the archives never to add to a growing body of advancing knowledge (which is exactly what I expect to happen to many of the "cognitive" studies being done today).

If the unification of psychology was a goal, unification research would become a part of the work of our science. Psychology shows that it is a preunified science by devoting all of its efforts to producing novel developments—new apparatuses and tests, new phenomena, "new" concepts and principles, new research findings, new therapies, new theories—and by expending almost no effort toward interrelating its developments. Under those circumstances—all production of new elements and no unification work—psychology can only become more and more diversified, specialized, complex, redundant, conflicting, and as a consequence more and more a would-be science and less and less a unified science.

Add these various conditions together and they spell chaotic knowledge, many times that of the early physics Kuhn described as where there are almost as many theories as important experimenters. Kuhn stated this earlier in the chapter. There is no belief that the limitlessly different phenomena of behavior that psychology studies will link together. So there is no search for that unification.

NEEDS OF THE MODERN PREUNIFIED SCIENCE

Early physics was a preunified science. It took great time and effort to make physics into a unified science. There is a common view that the way to make unified science is by composing a broad unified theory. It is the case that broad unified theory can interrelate a broad span of phenomena formerly considered different. But that belief in the singular importance of such theory is based on inadequate characterization of the preunified science. Having spent a career in crafting a wide-ranging, overarching, unified theory framework for psychology, let me suggest that there are many more tasks in unification of varying levels of complexity than that of composing a broad, overarching, unified theory. In psychology, because of the great expanse of phenomena and fields to be considered, such a theory can only be a framework, a guide, for the many such tasks of diverse kinds that must be carried out (see Staats, 1975, 1983, 1999). In illustration, take Kuhn's depiction of the morass of knowledge of electricity in the 1700s and the consensual theory of electricity and the various electrical phenomena that later emerged. Surely that development, a special area development, was fundamental to the later, broader unification of the phenomena of electricity, magnetism, and light that Shapere described. What I am suggesting is that attaining unified theory involves building unifications at lower levels and then at successively higher (broader) levels.

I am also suggesting that, as a preunified science, psychology must expend efforts in unifying lower level phenomena. Without that, construction of a grand unified theory is not possible. It would be easier to construct a theory of personality if the components were first unified. We have concepts such as self-confidence, self-esteem, self-efficacy, self, ego, ego-strength, and many more that share commonality. Would establishing that commonality in terms of underlying principles be helpful in constructing a unified theory of personality that involved a "self-type" concept. Of course. What are the various tasks of unification that will provide foundations for constructing progressively greater unification in psychology (see Darden & Maull, 1977; Staats, 1983, 1991, 1999)? Is this not one of the tasks that has to be considered in providing a platform for working toward unification? Psychology's unification represents a much greater problem than that which was involved for physics. And psychology has not begun the many other works that are needed to establish the many unifications that must be involved.

As has been indicated, the development from the preunified to the unified state of science takes a long time. My question is whether the process, and the time involved, can be short-circuited. Is it possible to create a "world view" that psychological phenomena are actually unified before the science itself has found a large number of unifications? Is it possible to change the way psychology operates, so that it assumes the characteristics of a unified science, before its unity findings have emerged? Is it possible to make the science receptive to looking for relationships—not just looking for novelty—for example, by creating journals and other media that reward the search for the various types of unification involved? If the advantages of being a unified science can be created before unification has been found, perhaps psychology can have the advantages of *operating* as a unified science in advance of its achievement of unified products.

Without such development, psychology will continue to multiply infinitely diverse studies done on its phenomena. Those studies may each be conducted with excellent scientific finesse. But if those studies do not hang together, are not woven into some common fabric of underlying principles, then they are only specific findings and do not provide a general picture (meaning). Worse, they will add to the puzzle of diversity. The scientists doing such work may be fully satisfied they are producing science. But actually they will set their science back in terms of unification. Their joint efforts will be evaluated as would-be science by those whose standards are of unified science.

Before psychology can be elevated to the pantheon of full science and be accepted, supported, and used by society as such, it must begin its march toward unification, toward deriving general meaning from the many unrelated studies it produces. There are many great works to be conducted in the unification effort—of philosophical, historical, theoretical, empirical, and methodological natures—in moving psychology along the disunity–unity dimension, in what will constitute a scientific revolution. When that has begun and progress has been made along that path, psychology's use in society and place in science will advance momentously. But getting that work underway is a great problem that needs the contributions of philosophers, historians, and sociologists of science as well as psychologists with various field interests. Let me suggest that these projections are relevant not only for psychology but for all preunified sciences.

CONCLUSION

I am sure that one day psychology will move in the unification direction, because nature is unified, including behavior, and I am convinced of the inevitability of this development for all sciences. That means that psychology too will one day become a unified science. I hope that at that time psychologists looking back, perhaps to this very book, will not say, "It is interesting that the problem of psychology's preunification was recognized a long time before the science even began working on the very evident and very important problem. That beginning was so important. Because once the first works showed the value of unifications in a few areas, unification became a dynamic. Then the various changes began to develop and those works accelerated, and the more that was done in the name of unification the more excitement was bred for doing more. That development then became a central effort, leading psychology to become a full science and providing a model for the other behavioral sciences to work on their problems of disunity. It is unfortunate the delay in beginning the work of unification held back psychology's basic and applied science development so long."

I began this analysis with my personal experience. Let me thus provide some closure in this respect. I continue to work on the advancement of my overarching unified theory, with its foundation constituted of smaller, underlying, unified theories in various areas along with their empirical and methodological developments. The elements (for the larger structure, see Staats, 1996) continue to be used, but in a piecemeal fashion, in specialty fields. That is justification enough for the overarching theory and the area developments. But the science still does not treat the broad, unified theory as such—does not analyze its positives and negatives, does not compare it and its methodology to other unified theories, does not test its implications, does not attempt to validate or invalidate it, and does not consider what unified theory must be like and must accomplish. These are all needed to provide knowledge for others to use in constructing overarching theories. But there is no tradition for such works in psychology. That is even true of theories with lesser scope (such as personality theories, psychotherapy theories, child development theories, theories of aspects of cognition). They, too, are not systematically considered with the goal of building a more coherent science. It is as though such theories, and works in psychology in general, are free to occur as separate entities. There is no goal of building a unified, coherent structure of science. So there is no understanding of how to exploit a broad unified theory or how to advance it or evaluate it. At present a unified theory is like a tree that falls in a forest where there is no one. The tree makes sound waves, but no noise, for there is no one to hear. Before psychology makes the noise of a full science, psychologists will have to become aware of the forest and enter it to begin to working in that forest the various tasks of unification.

REFERENCES

Bijou, S. W. (1957). Methodology for the experimental analysis of child behavior. *Psychological Reports, 3*, 243–250.

Boneau, A. C. (1988). Making psychology useful: A framework for understanding human action. *International Newsletter of Uninomic Psychology, 6*, 1–13.

Cofer, C. N., & Foley, J. P. (1942). Mediated generalization and the interpretation of verbal behavior: I. Prolegomena. *Psychological Review, 49*, 513–540.

Darden, L., & Maull, N. (1977). Interfield theory. *Philosophy of Science, 44*, 43–64.

Deese, J. (1959). On the prediction of occurrence of particular verbal intrusions in immediate recall. *Journal of Experimental Psychology, 58*, 17–22.

Dollard, J., & Miller, N. E. (1950). *Personality and psychotherapy*. New York: McGraw-Hill.

Doob, L. W. (1947). The behavior of attitudes. *Psychological Review, 54*, 135–156.

Driver-Linn, E. (2003). Where is psychology going: Structural fault lines revealed by psychologists' use of Kuhn. *American Psychologist, 58*, 269–278.

Gaston, J. (1973). *Originality and competition in science*. Chicago: University of Chicago Press.

Hull, C. L. (1920). Quantitative aspects of the evolution of concepts. *Psychological Monographs, 123*.

Kimble, G. A. (1997). A frame of reference for psychology. *American Psychologist, 49*, 510–519.

Koch, S. (1981). The nature and limits of psychological knowledge. *American Psychologist, 36*, 257–259.

Kuhn, T. S. (1962). *The structure of scientific revolutions* (2nd ed.). Chicago: University of Chicago Press.

Lindsley, O. R. (1956). Operant conditioning methods applied to research in chronic schizophrenia. *Psychiatric Research Reports, 5*, 140–153.

Maltzman, I. (1955). Thinking: From a behaviorist point of view. *Psychological Review, 62*, 275–286.

Merton, R. K. (1957). Priorities in scientific discovery. *American Sociological Review, 22*, 635–659.

Nagel, E. (1961). *The structure of science*. New York: Harcourt, Brace, and World.

Osgood, C. E. (1953). *Method and theory in experimental psychology*. New York: Oxford University Press.

Ravetz, J. R. (1971). *Scientific knowledge and its social problems*. Oxford, England: Clarendon Press.

Russell, W. A., & Storms, L. H. (1955). Implicit verbal chaining in paired-associate learning. *Journal of Experimental Psychology, 49*, 287–293.

Shapere, D. (1977). Scientific theories and their domains. In F. Suppe (Ed.), *The structure of scientific theories* (2nd ed., pp. 518–565). Urbana: University of Illinois Press.

Shapere, D. (1979). *The character of scientific change*. Unpublished manuscript.

Skinner, B. F. (1953). *Science and human behavior*. New York: Macmillan.

Skinner, B. F. (1957). *Verbal behavior*. New York: Appleton.

Staats, A. W. (with contributions by C. K. Staats). (1963). *Complex human behavior*. New York: Holt, Rinehart & Winston.

Staats, A. W. (1968). Social behaviorism and human motivation: Principles of the attitude–reinforcer–discriminative system. In A. G. Greenwald, T. C. Brock, & T. M. Ostrom (Eds.), *Psychological foundations of attitudes* (pp. 33–66). New York: Academic Press.

Staats, A. W. (1970). A learning–behavior theory: A basis for unity in behavioral-social science. In A. R. Gilgen (Ed.), *Contemporary scientific psychology* (pp. 183–239). New York: Academic Press.

Staats, A. W. (1975). *Social behaviorism*. Homewood, IL: Dorsey Press.

Staats, A. W. (1981). Psychological behaviorism, unified theory, unified theory construction, and the Zeitgeist of separatism. *American Psychologist, 36*, 239–256.

Staats, A. W. (1983). *Psychology's crisis of disunity: Philosophy and method for a unified science*. New York: Praeger.

Staats, A. W. (1987). Unified positivism: Philosophy for the revolution to unity. In A. W. Staats & L. P. Mos (Eds.), *Annals of theoretical psychology* (Vol. 5, pp. 11–54). New York: Plenum Press.

Staats, A. W. (1991). Unified positivism and unified psychology: Fad or new field? *American Psychologist, 46,* 899–912.

Staats, A. W. (1996). *Behavior and personality: Psychological behaviorism.* New York: Springer.

Staats, A. W. (1999). Unifying psychology requires new infrastructure, theory, methods, and research agenda. *Review of General Psychology, 3,* 3–13.

Stevens, S. S. (1951). *Handbook of experimental psychology.* New York: Wiley.

Toulmin, S. (1972). *Human understanding.* Princeton, NJ: Princeton University Press.

Tryon, W. W. (1990). Why paradigmatic behaviorism should be retitled psychological behaviorism. *Behavior Therapist, 13,* 127–128.

Watson, J. B. (1930). *Behaviorism* (Rev. ed.). Chicago: University of Chicago Press.

INDEX

Evidence-based practice, 6–7
Evolutionary psychology, 79, 107
Excitation, 100–101
Experience, 92, 100
Experimental psychology, 159–160, 172
Explanatory function, 92–93

Fallibilist privilege, 34
Faust, Jan, 111–112
Fordham Institute for Innovations in
    Social Policy, 115
Fordham Social Health Index, 115–116
Forensic psychology, 108
Fragmentation, 4, 5–13, 21–22, 69
Frank, Jerome, 54
Free speech, 6
Freud, Sigmund, 82–83
Frye, Northrup, 41
Functional behaviorism, 104

Galileo, 164–165
Geisteswissenschaften, 28, 32, 33
Gender studies, 107
Geropsychology, 108
Graduate psychology core courses, 24
Grant funding, 5

Hall, G. Stanley, 64
Hardiness, 120
Harvard Project Zero, 85
Health and Behavior codes, 112
Health and Human Services (HHS),
    Department of, 109
Health care, 109–112
Health psychology, 108, 111–112
Health risk factors, 110
Hebb, Donald, 86
Hebephrenic speech, 96
Hermeneutics, 32
Hull, Clark, 45–46, 48, 148
Human sciences, 26
Humanities, 27–29

Identity crisis, 87
Ignorance, 4
Inhibition, 100–101
Input–output feedback, 154

Institutes of Medicine (IOM), 109
Instrumental conditioning, 162
Intellectual property protection,
    165–166
Intelligence, types of, 93
Interpersonal psychodynamic therapy,
    56
Intersociety Constitutional Committee,
    70
Interventions, 110–111
Involuntary action, 96–97
Iraq, 119, 139
Ironic vision, 43–44

James, Henry, 83
James–Lange theory, 93
James, William, 78, 82–83, 87, 88, 101
Journal–databases, 51

Kendler, H. W., 153, 155, 162
Kimble, Gregory, 162
Koch, Sigmund, 62, 78, 162
Kuhn, T. S., 126
Kulik, J., 130, 131

Ladd, George, 64
Lashley, Karl, 87
Learning theory, 97
Linguistic solopsism, 34
Literature, 84–85
Logical positivism, 33

Mature sciences, 18
Memory, 93
Mental health care, 110
Method, 146–147, 152–154
Michigan Conference, 130
Military prescriptive privileges, 8, 10
Military psychologists, 112–115
Miller, James G., 46–47, 48
Mind, brain, and education (MBE), 78,
    82
Morrill Land-Grant Act, 128
Mortality, 110
Motivation, 93
Multicultural psychology, 108
Murray, Henry A., 83, 84

ABOUT THE EDITOR

Robert J. Sternberg, PhD, is best known for his theory of successful intelligence, investment theory of creativity (developed with Todd Lubart), theory of mental self-government, balance theory of wisdom as well as for his triangular theory of love and theory of love as a story. The focus of his research is intelligence and cognitive development. He is the author of more than 800 journal articles, book chapters, and books and has received about $15 million in government grants and contracts for his research. He is past-president of the American Psychological Association (APA) and former editor of *Contemporary Psychology*. He received his PhD from Stanford University in 1975 and his BA *summa cum laude*, Phi Beta Kappa, from Yale University in 1972. He has won many awards, including the Early Career Award from the APA, Outstanding Book Awards from the American Educational Research Association, the Distinguished Lifetime Contribution to Psychology Award from the Connecticut Psychological Association, the Cattell Award of the Society for Multivariate Experimental Psychology, and the Award for Excellence of the Mensa Education and Research Foundation. He has held a Guggenheim Fellowship as well as Yale University Senior and Junior Faculty Fellowships. He has been president of several APA divisions, including the Society for General Psychology (Division 1); the Society for the Psychology of Aesthetics, Creativity, and the Arts (Division 10); Educational Psychology (Division 15); and Theoretical and Philosophical Psychology (Division 24). He has also served as editor of the *Psychological Bulletin*.

DATE DUE

5/1/06			
MAY 0 1 2016			